“So many Christians have fallen
order to build up the church and
we need to pretend to be stron
weak, and Hindley urges us all to come clean and admit our weakness—and to let it drive us to the One who is strong. The book is itself a lovely illustration of its own message: it is full of honest and illuminating examples from the author’s own life.

I hope lots of church leaders will read and take this book to heart. If they do, then church life will be very different: churches will be beautiful places where people are set free to humbly depend on one another and on the Lord in ways that really build up the church and point a watching world to the glory of One whose ‘power is made perfect in weakness.’”

Mike Cain, church minister and author of *Real-Life Jesus*

“John Hindley’s honesty is refreshing, relatable, and real as he humbly shares his personal illustrations of weakness. But he also shows us how Christ’s own experience of weakness can strengthen us. This book is a comfort, a reassurance, and a beautiful reminder that ‘weakness can be a route into the very heart of God.’ A brilliant book! And very easy to read too. It definitely gave voice to some of my own thoughts as I wrestled with my own weakness.”

Ruth Clemence, writer, blogger at ruthclemence.com, podcaster, and book reviewer

"In an age that can over-value the strong and stigmatise the weak, John Hindley identifies the imposter in all of us that can appear competent but fears exposure. The fact is that we are needy, and this book leads us to the One we desperately need. What a relief!

This book is biblical, readable, and accessible to all levels within a church community. It will probe your relationship to your own weaknesses, both as a sufferer and a sinner. Whilst helpful at an individual level, it would be an immensely beneficial book for a church to read together. At a time when stress and weariness are particular struggles in the body of Christ, and resilience much sought after, John Hindley leads us to depend on a slain Lamb who is also the power and wisdom of God. Through personal illustration too, we see how the Lord works surprising strength through our weaknesses.

Highly recommended for both personal and corporate strengthening."

Andrew Collins, Certificate Course Director,
Biblical Counselling UK; biblical counsellor and
former consultant psychiatrist

"*Weakness Our Strength.* What a strange title in a world that hates weakness and hides it behind all sorts of masks! John Hindley admirably shows us how this divine paradox is inevitably linked to our growth into Christlikeness: God's power is made perfect not so much in spite of our weaknesses, but through them.

I am very impressed by the way Hindley connects the truths

of the Bible with everyday life. His practical and thought-provoking style makes *Weakness Our Strength* a source of inspiration and personal renewal."

Pablo Martinez, psychiatrist, conference speaker,
and author of *A Thorn in the Flesh*

"Could another book on weakness actually say something 'new under the sun'? Something that will help sufferers like me who struggle with pain and paralysis? If you assume there's nothing fresh to write about our weakness, God's strength, and the connection between them, then think again. John Hindley's newest release, *Weakness Our Strength*, will utterly surprise you. Perhaps it's his own journey on the tender, yet torturous path to the cross, a road many Christians are reticent to even tread. It could be the way he handles the subject like a prism, refracting gospel-light to reveal hues and shades of truth we've never noticed before. I can't say. But I know this: the author has a way of gently taking the walking wounded by the hand and placing that hand on the Saviour's heart. It's why I love this book and am commending it to everyone for whom weakness is a way of life.

Thank you, John Hindley; I give your newest work my hearty recommendation."

Joni Eareckson Tada, Joni and Friends International Disability Center; conference speaker, author, and artist

"The idea that our Maker intended us to be limited, and even weak, seems counter-intuitive to modern ears, and perhaps even dangerous. But my overarching sensation while reading John Hindley's new book was one of immense relief. He says nothing that will be unfamiliar to readers of the Bible, but he brings deep personal experience, and above all honesty, to bear on what can be a very difficult subject, which is what makes this book so refreshing.

If all the leaders of our churches and organisations took even half of what this book teaches to heart, then they would be very different places: safe, open communities where those all too aware of their own weakness and failings need not fear getting crushed by the perfectionism, bravado or facades of so much of church life. I'm immensely grateful to John for this book!"

Mark Meynell, Director (Europe & Caribbean), Langham Preaching; author of *When Darkness Seems My Closest Friend* and *What Angels Long to Read*

WEAKNESS OUR STRENGTH

LEARNING FROM CHRIST CRUCIFIED

JOHN HINDLEY

Union Publishing

Weakness Our Strength

www.UnionPublishing.org
Bridgend, Wales, United Kingdom

Cover design by Rubner Durais

978-1-9168995-8-2 (paperback)
978-1-9168995-9-9 (eBook)

For Felicity, my wife.

For twenty years now, the Lord Jesus has been teaching us how weakness together, with him and with one another, is true strength. Thank you for your godly love, wisdom, kindness, and so much fun.

And for Daisy, Eliza, and Sylvia, and for the other children who are, and have been, part of our family. You share your weaknesses with me, accept mine, and teach me so much about our God. Family life is hectic and hilarious, often leaving me bewildered, and Jesus is very kind in it all.

CONTENTS

FROM THE AUTHOR

I don't want to admit that I am weak. And I don't want you to think that my weakness makes me admirable.

Those two reasons are why I am quite nervous about this book. The second one is more dangerous than the first.

Let's get the first one out of the way. I am a weak man. I read an article about the *Beano* comic a couple of years ago in which a member of its publishing staff claimed that readers were generally not like Dennis the Menace, the character whose villainous exploits have been at the heart of the comic for years. Rather, they were generally more like Walter the Softie, Dennis's nemesis. As a boy, I read the *Beano* and, unsurprisingly according to the article, regularly felt sorry for Walter as Dennis terrorised him and his chums yet again.

As a teenager, I read books about Hornblower[1] and fantasy

1 Horatio Hornblower is a fictional British naval officer serving during the Napoleonic Wars. C. S. Forester wrote a series of novels and short stories detailing his career.

heroes like Druss the Legend.[2] Men of action, courage, and strong compassion. Alongside that, I was deeply envious of schoolmates who were anything like them, which I was not. I played Warhammer rather than football, and stayed in on a Friday night. I hoped that one day I would grow up to find that overnight I had become a hero, a man of action, a rugged and dependable husband, father, and friend. One day.

As I have written this book, Jesus has shown me my weakness in its true colours. It runs even more deeply and sadly than I had realised, and I do not like it. I have tried to weave some of this into what follows, and I have to admit that it makes me squirm a bit! I am not the only weak one, though. The backdrop to writing this book was something that none of us could have imagined: a global humbling.

Remember the coronavirus pandemic, when the strength of the world was humbled by a virus? Entire nations, businesses, schools, and churches were brought to a standstill in confusion and fear. We were brought low, and we are still reaping the whirlwind of anxiety, fear, depression, and loss that we sowed with arrogant confidence in our technology, wisdom, and power.

At the same time, the strength of some more conservative parts of the church, where I am perhaps most at home, was also humbled by the public fall of certain well-respected leaders and preachers. All parts of the church have, sadly, been affected in similar ways. Sexual scandals, the use of ministry for personal

2 See, for example, David Gemmell, *Legend* (London: Century, 1984). Here we first meet Druss as a veteran warrior who comes out of retirement to help lead the heroic defence of his nation against a fearsome and vast enemy horde.

enrichment, the abuse of power—all with consequent casualties—and the confusion over what is fair and not fair unfolded at a bewildering pace. Friends were involved in some of these public matters, so it all landed very close to home. Alongside all of this, I was also directly involved in several lesser-known situations involving friends, sometimes in dispute with one another. (I feel sick as I bring these matters to mind now.) Some issues were resolved, others not, and a lot of people are left deeply wounded. We have been confused, broken, unsure, questioning the Lord. In a word, weak.

Tired from helping to lead a church during a pandemic, and sad and confused by the hurt in other churches, I experienced weakness even closer up, too, as I wrote. My wife Flick (short for Felicity) and I had become foster carers, a role which continues to show us both the weakness of families where abuse and neglect are endemic and the weakness of a system struggling to cope with the scale of harm being done to children. Fostering has also shown up our own weakness as a couple as we have tried to love Christ, one another, our birth children, our foster children, and our church family. We are often far beyond ourselves, and so slow to depend on the loving help around us from our God and our brothers and sisters.

Over the past several months, I have been frustrated, angry, despairing, and downcast more often, and more deeply, maybe, than I have ever been before. Yet I still long to be strong. I do not want to be Hornblower anymore, but now I envy husbands who know just how to show love to their wives in timely and wise ways. I envy fathers who are unflappably patient and full of grace towards their children. I envy pastors who seem to have all the answers their churches need, and who lead people to Christ both effortlessly and often. I feel like an inadequate imposter in my life; I feel weak, and I do not like it.

I wonder, though, if Jesus has let me experience this weakness and see it more closely so that I can write this book? He has certainly drawn me close to himself and soothed my heart chapter by chapter. So this is a raw work, written in weakness. And frankly, I think that is a good thing.

My second concern is the one that bothers me a lot more than the above—namely, whether I have written too much about myself, and in a misleading way. I am worried that I have made too much of myself, and even displayed myself in a flattering light. My weakness is not noble. Indeed, much of it is sin, which is ugly, and some of the rest is from being a fallen man in a fallen world, which is miserable. The problem is that writing about weakness, and using my own weakness as an example, can make it seem as though I am admirably self-aware, wisely searching the Scriptures for the help I need, and faithfully bringing my every need to our heavenly Father. If only!

It is a dangerous thing to write about myself because I might lead your gaze to me, John, rather than to Jesus. If I do that, it will do you no good, make me a sinner, and snatch glory from the kindest and most glorious Lord. Thankfully, God has given me a wife, fellow elders, friends, and an editor to lead me out of that swamp. But a beautiful self-portrait might peek through at times. If it does, please know that my sin is not noble; it is nasty, and my weakness is not brave; it is brutal.

But Jesus is noble. He is brave, kind, generous, and full of grace. He is our hope, strength, and song. Jesus is also the One who makes sense of our weakness, as we will see, in ways that surprise us. He is Lord and Saviour. Jesus is all.

And one day our weakness will be over and forgotten—forever.

John Hindley

Frettenham, Norfolk, September 2022

1

We Are Weak

I came into Norwich early this morning to spend the day writing. As I ordered breakfast in a local pub, the manager asked me what I was doing. So I told him that I was writing a book about weakness, and how Jesus knows that we are weak and does not expect us to sort ourselves out before we come to him. He said that he reckoned it was a good subject, because everyone who comes into his pub is "fine." They all tell him they are doing well. And then sometimes they tell him the truth. My guess is that a publican hears a fair bit of the truth after a couple of beers.

The truth is that we are barely holding it together, at best. We are weak, and our weakness is painful. Some of that weakness is obvious. We cannot hide the weakness of ill health, whether it be the grinding weakness of chronic illness or the terrible weakness that cancer brings, both in the disease and its consequent treatments. When it is family who are suffering, the weakness and confusion can feel even worse than when we are suffering ourselves. When those we love have died, the pain and grief often come with a sense of confusion and powerlessness. Our family and friends rally round us, as they know something of this suffering too. Or maybe they don't, and our grief is made worse by loneliness and isolation. When we lose our job, or the bank takes our house, those around us cannot fail to notice how weak we are and how hard life is for us.

Much of our weakness is hidden, though. I have been careful in how I have talked about the panic attack that I had. And I hardly know how to begin talking about the anxiety that lurks just beneath the surface. I am not sure exactly what I am anxious about, although my worry may fix on a random item on my to-do list or an entry in my diary. Sometimes I feel so downcast and dejected that I struggle to get out of bed or do anything much when I have got up. Yet for me, these things are neither constant nor total. So my weakness is part of my experience but not the whole, and that somehow makes it hard to discuss with friends whilst keeping some sense of perspective.

Then there is the weakness that lingers on the borders between suffering and sin. On busy days, when I have worked hard and still ended up moving three tasks onto tomorrow's long list, I finish by feeling overwhelmed, inadequate, frustrated with myself and anyone else I can think of—even with the Lord. I fight a rising anger that threatens to come out in cruel and unfair words to my children, or coldness and distance towards my wife.

I sometimes feel as though Christ has loaded too much onto my plate. Sometimes I even tell him so and ask him for his help. Too frequently, though, I simply wish that I were better, that I were stronger, that I were more gifted, more disciplined, with a higher capacity to work and less need for sleep. I want to be more like other Christians I know who have everything sorted out and time for all the Lord has called them to do. They're calm and collected in the face of pressure and able to get far more done than I am, before enjoying stimulating and creative rest. Instead of just slumping on the sofa.

The strange thing is that I suspect that if you met me, you would think I was just that sort of Christian too! Which makes me wonder whether the people I look up to, and sinfully envy, are maybe more like me than they first appear. I wonder if the pub manager is right that we all pretend to enjoy a greater strength than we have. Maybe we are like the man I read about who had got so fed up with the effort of trying to develop a rippling six-pack through his workouts at the gym that he simply had one tattooed on instead. I smiled as I recognised something of myself in him.

I am weak, and you are too. You are probably reading this book because you feel the exhaustion and frustration of being a weak person in a world that loves strength. You are confused. You struggle to find a place when you see so many Christians and churches radiating calm, control, strength, peace, and joy. Alongside them, or as part of such a church, you feel that you do not fit in. You feel so empty, broken, messed up, and downright sinful. You are wondering why, if God is mighty, powerful, and on your side, things are proving so hard. Maybe you simply cannot keep the bills down; you are unable to imagine an end to the depression; your child has cancer, and you do not know how it will end. Perhaps you suspect the world sees you as strong, coping, competent, and together, and you cannot work out how to mention your daily addiction, mental illness, inner emptiness, or shallow faith to anyone. You feel trapped in an image you have created, as the gulf between the truth of who you are and the impression you give to others widens every week.

So it helps you to know that I too am weak, just as it helps me to know that you are. This book is not written by the strong to help the strong get stronger. Nor is it written by the strong to help the weak. A friend suggested the book could be called *A Weakling's Guide to Weakness*, and he was right! I am weak, and being weak, I understand something of weakness. The hope, though, is not that I might understand something of *your* weakness. Rather, the sure and certain hope is that your Father in heaven understands your weakness; he understands it perfectly:

> As a father shows compassion to his children,
> so the LORD shows compassion to those who fear him.
> For he knows our frame;
> he remembers that we are dust. (Ps. 103:13–14)

The Lord remembers that we are but dust. He has no false expectations of us, no demands that we cannot meet, and no standards that we must achieve. He is more compassionate than the best of earthly fathers is with his children. Our God knows that we are weak; he knows the struggles we face and the burdens we bear. He knows how we simply cannot keep going, and that we need to relax our grip and lower our mask of successful strength. That is why Jesus came to call us, with words like these:

> Come to me, all who labor and are heavy laden, and I will give you rest. Take my yoke upon you, and learn from me, for I am gentle and lowly in heart, and you will find rest for your souls. For my yoke is easy, and my burden is light. (Matt. 11:28–30)

Jesus is not a God who expects us to grow stronger backs and broader shoulders for him to lay more burdens on. He is a God who offers to take our burdens from us and carry them for us. He knows what we cannot bear, and he came so that we would no longer have to bear it. Jesus knows us and comes alongside us. He offers us a seat, pours us a drink, and sits down himself. His very eyes tell us that he understands, and his outstretched hands let us know that he has come to help. The scars from the nails remind us just how far his love goes. Here is One in whom we will find rest for our souls.

We can come with our weakness to Jesus. We can come to learn from him, for he is not strong in the ways in which we long to be strong; rather, he is gentle and lowly in heart. He is weak, but he is strong also, and we will never understand his strength unless we understand his weakness. For it was in the weakness of a child that God came to us, and in the ultimate weakness of a broken body and a death in the darkness that God saved us.

We see Christ most truly if we see him in the weakness of his cross. It is by seeing this cross that we can understand how our weakness is not something to be avoided, escaped from, or concealed. We will see that our weakness can be a route into the very heart of God, a way of freedom and an invitation to know rest in our souls.

2

Christ Crucified: The Heart of Weakness and Strength

I hear the Saviour say,
"Thy strength indeed is small.
Child of weakness, watch and pray,
Find in me thine all in all."

Jesus paid it all,
All to him I owe.
Sin had left a crimson stain;
He washed it white as snow.

Elvina M. Hall, "Jesus Paid It All," 1865

Ragged, outnumbered, bone-weary, and seemingly doomed, the defenders of Dros Delnoch gather on the walls before the countless hordes of the Nadir. They are led by Druss, a legend in his lifetime but now in his sixties, and Regnak the Wanderer, who has already avoided battle due to his lack of courage. Despite their fears and doubts, they stand ready on the walls. They defy the odds and choose to hope in the face of despair.

With such stories, David Gemmell captured my heart as a teenager longing for glory.[1] As you now know, I love stories with legendary heroes, as many of us do. I enjoy books and films with good, strong warriors fighting against evil and for those who cannot fight for themselves.

None of the heroes whose stories I admire is alone. There is always a band, a group, or a team. Think of Luke, Leia, and Han from Star Wars or the Nine Companions of J. R. R. Tolkien's Fellowship of the Ring. To be strong, they rely on one another.

When we know we are weak, perhaps our desire to depend on others is greater. We see our need, and we see how others can meet it. We like the idea of being part of the heroic band.

Here is a thought that encourages me in my Christian walk: Jesus will draw us into his band; he will share his glory with us. There is something right in our desire for this. But there is a problem too. Before we can share the strength of Christ, we have to understand weakness: we have to see both our weakness and his weakness. We have to see that we are needy and not the heroes we'd dearly like to be.

It is through showing us our need that the Holy Spirit draws us to Jesus. He convicts the world "concerning sin and righteousness and judgment" (John 16:8). The Spirit shows us that we are sinners and that we cannot save ourselves. We are guilty, facing God's anger and judgement, and we need to be

1 See David Gemmell, *Legend* (London: Century, 1984).

rescued. This is hard for us to hear, because it requires us to see ourselves as weak. We are not heroes, but rather the ones who need rescuing. And we really do have to see how needy we are, because only then will we be able to recognise, with joy and wonder, just how good and necessary Jesus' rescue is.

Helpless in our sin

Before Christ died to save us, we were as weak as it was possible to be, utterly unable to do anything to help ourselves. We were at our weakest when it came to sin and salvation, like a person adrift in a stormy sea, miles from any help. In fact, our plight was even worse than that, for Paul says, "You were dead in the trespasses and sins in which you once walked" (Eph. 2:1). So we were not just in danger of drowning in a storm of sin; we were already dead.

Paul calls us "dead," and this captures just how shockingly helpless we were.

In saving us, Christ does not give a helping hand to people trying hard to live holy lives. He does not even give an essential shove to those who need someone to get them going. Christ gives life to the dead. We are so incapable of saving ourselves, returning to God's love, and gaining entry to his kingdom that we are dead.

A helplessness we deserve

Even more shockingly, we deserve this condition of being helpless in death. We tend to think of our sin as a light matter, something thrust upon us that is not really our fault. I tend to view my selfishness and meanness not as coming out of me, but as forced upon me by the stress and suffering of life.

A couple of days ago, my wife and I were going through our diaries to mark off some times to spend together. As I kept explaining why this time or that time was impossible because of the work I needed to do, I became increasingly frustrated, and I took it out on Flick by blaming her for being uncaring about the pressure I was under. I knew I was sinning against her, but I was feeling trapped in a corner by busyness, tiredness, and even by Christ, whose work I was aiming to do. I felt that I was trying my best, and so the sin could not be my fault. Yet it was.

This selfishness and unkindness rose up from inside me. Flick was not putting me in a difficult position, far less Jesus. I was simply feeling frustrated at my lack of control over the world. I was acting as though I was a god who should be in control. And this is offensive to the true God, who is full of care and kindness. We have turned away from the One who is life and goodness, love and grace. By our own efforts, we have earned death and the judgement of hell for our sins.

This is hard to stomach. Hard because this is not how I like to think about myself. I like to think that I am a good person. Yet I am very quick to do, and to justify, what works out best for me and gets me the ease, respect, and applause that I feel I deserve and crave. This is what it feels like to be dead in our sins. But then we read words of hope:

> But God, being rich in mercy, because of the great love

> with which he loved us, even when we were dead in our trespasses, made us alive together with Christ—by grace you have been saved. (Eph. 2:4–5)

Jesus does not choose the best players for his team, and he does not choose the sorted, the strong, and the successful either. God sets his great love on us simply because he loves us. He did everything we needed because of love, not because we deserved it. Not one bit!

Christ's glorious weakness

Christ took on our weakness in total and terrible love in a human body. As he approached his death, he prayed, "Father, the hour has come; glorify your Son that the Son may glorify you" (John 17:1). The cross was the hour of God's glory, and it is here that we see God most glorified, most truly and clearly revealed. The cross was a mighty victory: Jesus defeated the awesome power of sin, death, and the devil. Yet here was a victory won in weakness.

Now, let's be clear: there is certainly strength in Christ's cross, strength in his obedience to death, and strength in his resurrection. This is to say nothing of the power we see in him or his creation, or in the authority of his Word. Yet that strength is not ashamed to be weak. In fact, that strength is seen most clearly in the weakness of the cross, as we noted above. Writing of the message of the cross that he preaches, the apostle Paul says,

> For Jews demand signs and Greeks seek wisdom, but we preach Christ crucified, a stumbling block to Jews and folly to Gentiles, but to those who are called, both Jews and Greeks, Christ the power of God and the wisdom of God. For the foolishness of God is wiser than men, and the weakness of God is stronger than men. (1 Cor. 1:22–25)

Christ's cross is both weakness and strength. It is God's weakness, which is stronger than man's strength. The weakness of the cross is very obvious: Jesus puts himself in the hands of powerful and evil men who condemn him to death in a mockery of a trial. He then submits to the authority of a weak Roman governor who would rather appease a crowd baying for blood than release a man he knows to be innocent. This is the sort of weakness that we see on the news all the time: dictators and cowards conniving to remove inconvenient opponents through callous soldiers and volatile mobs.

Having been condemned, Jesus is beaten, insulted, humiliated, and finally killed by being nailed to a cross. Hanging naked under the scorn and mockery of his enemies, he was abandoned by most of his friends, betrayed by one and denied by another. Dying, he took on himself the weight of his people's sin and suffered the judgement of God. His Father poured out holy wrath on his dear Son, and heaven trembled as Christ drank the cup.

In utter darkness, Jesus breathed his last and gave up his Spirit, declaring, "It is finished" (John 19:30). He broke every claim that sin, death, or Satan has on us. He died for sinners like us, and sinners like us are now forgiven; those dead and lost are found and made alive. This is both the greatest victory and the most humiliating weakness that has ever been, or will ever be, known.

Jesus' broken and scarred corpse was carried by two friends to a borrowed tomb (John 19:38–42). Picture the bitter tears as Joseph and Nicodemus struggle to carry the blood-stained, battered body of their Saviour across the execution ground. With defeat in their hearts and gore on their hands, they stagger towards the nearby tomb in bleak and terrible grief.

Jesus is dead, completely beyond any ability to do anything for himself, humiliated, and, it seems, finished. Everything we would value in any way has been stripped from him in a death calculated to leave nothing.

This is what we fear: losing everything. Yet Jesus lost everything, and so whatever we fear losing in our weakness, he lost too. Perhaps we value the strength of wealth, possessions, security, and ease. Soldiers gambled for Jesus' clothes, the last things he owned, as he died. Perhaps we value success, productivity, and achievement. As he died, it seemed outwardly as though everything was over for him, that his great mission and ministry had ended in abject failure. Perhaps we value reputation, fame, and applause. But in the end, everyone abandoned Jesus to his fate, from the crowds who shouted for his death to his friends who failed to stand by him. In whatever ways we feel, and fear, weakness, Christ felt it too. Here is the weakness of God unashamedly laid bare.

We face no weakness that takes us beyond Jesus. Sitting in the dark, alone in my study, unable even to cry and paralysed by my fears, I have never been able to escape him. I cannot go deeper into weakness than Jesus went. Weakness has no cranny he does not know. There is no place I can run to where Jesus cannot find me, no darkness so great that he cannot ride into it with flaming torch to carry me home. We need a strong Saviour; we need a weak one too.

Christ's unbreakable strength

On that execution ground, we also see the strength of God, a strength far stronger than ours. It must also be a different strength from that for which we strive, for the strength of God, true strength, is a gifted and a dependent strength.

Talking of laying down his life for his sheep, Jesus says,

> For this reason the Father loves me, because I lay down my life that I may take it up again. No one takes it from me, but I lay it down of my own accord. I have authority to lay it down, and I have authority to take it up again. This charge I have received from my Father. (John 10:17–18)

Jesus laid down his life by his own authority. Neither the ruling council of priests and elders nor the governor from Rome had authority over the King of Kings unless it was given to them by God (John 19:11). Jesus was obedient to death on a cross (Phil. 2:8) because he was obedient to his Father, and it was his Father who gave him the authority to lay down his own life. So the weakness that he took on voluntarily was a weakness given by his Father. But it was also a gift of glory.

Christ's glory is the display of his love, grace, and truth. It is to be the One whom the nations worship. It is to be worthy of all praise and honour because he has saved us freely and in love. We get a sense of Christ's glory as God, his Father, addresses him in Isaiah 49:6:

> It is too light a thing that you should be my servant
>   to raise up the tribes of Jacob
>   and to bring back the preserved of Israel;
> I will make you as a light for the nations,
>   that my salvation may reach to the end of the earth.

The Father wanted his Son to receive the glory of being the selflessly loving Saviour of Israel and of all the nations. Christ is the Lamb who was slain, the One who gave himself for us, and that love and sacrifice is his glory. His weakness is his strength, and his Father gave him that weak strength to honour him.

I am embarrassed to confess here that I am often ashamed of the weakness of Jesus. When friends challenge me that if God really was God, he would work a miracle "right now," I feel that he should! I wish Jesus had the sort of power a genie has—exerting mighty strength for me at one rub of the lamp. That is not his way, however. He brings us to share his glory through suffering, producing joy through sorrow and hope in trials. We've seen how his strength was shown and known in weakness. He draws us into the light of that glory, but the only way in is through weakness.

Christ's was also a strength that was dependent on his Father. Repeatedly in the book of Acts, his early followers declared that Jesus had risen. They did so as proof of his kingly authority, which demanded that their hearers bow before this mighty Lord. As Peter declared on the day of Pentecost,

> This Jesus God raised up, and of that we all are witnesses. Being therefore exalted at the right hand of God, and having received from the Father the promise of the Holy Spirit, he has poured out this that you yourselves are seeing and hearing. … Let all the house of Israel therefore know for certain that God has made him both Lord and Christ, this Jesus whom you crucified. (Acts 2:32–33, 36)

Christ's authority to lay down his life and take it up again was given by his Father. As God raised him up from death and exalted him to his right hand, he showed Jesus truly to be "both Lord and Christ." This means that the strength of Christ is a dependent strength: Jesus knew that his Father was completely faithful and would raise him up from the dead. God is strong together, not alone.

So then, as I sit in my study brooding over my suffering and nursing my hurts, I can know that Christ has gone down further into weakness than I ever will go. And so he is well able to come and find me. But crucially, he has also risen in life-giving strength. And so he is also well able to raise me up, to take me to life in God. Weaker than my weakness, Jesus is also far stronger than my strength.

Strength in weakness

Yesterday I moved some furniture: chairs, a lamp, and side tables that I was perfectly able to shift by myself. But there were also mattresses and sofas that were simply too heavy and bulky for me to manage. My friend Matthew has a lot of experience in moving furniture and packing a van, so we worked together. With the two of us, and especially with Matthew's expertise, there was nothing that was too tricky to shift. Whereas one of us working alone was too weak to do the job, working together we were strong. I was weak; we were strong. This is the nature of godly weakness and godly strength.

While we long to be strong in ourselves, independent, and self-sufficient, God's strength is a mutual strength, expressed in relationship and in dependence. To fully enjoy this mutual strength requires weakness. Throughout the Bible, we see the partnership of God the Father, God the Son, and God the Holy Spirit: the three persons of the Holy Trinity always acting in unity and in harmony, relying on one another. God is strong together as Trinity, and the three persons delight in their mutual interdependence—they don't act independently.

In a good sense, human weakness and strength will always follow the same pattern as God's: I am weak; we are strong. This is how weakness and strength relate as we come to

Christ. And we will go on following him in exactly this way, as children like their Father.

Children and heirs

After he rose from the dead, Christ returned to heaven to take his place at his Father's side. From there he sent the Holy Spirit to us, to lead us through life:

> For all who are led by the Spirit of God are sons of God. For you did not receive the spirit of slavery to fall back into fear, but you have received the Spirit of adoption as sons, by whom we cry, "Abba! Father!" The Spirit himself bears witness with our spirit that we are children of God, and if children, then heirs—heirs of God and fellow heirs with Christ, provided we suffer with him in order that we may also be glorified with him. (Rom. 8:14–17)

Here we read the almost unbelievable truth that we are children of God. The Holy Spirit made us one with Jesus as he died. He has united us to him more closely than a bride to her husband so that our sin can truly be his; he can carry it down to death. The Spirit has also united us to Christ so that he can share with us the relationship he enjoys with his Father, God.

God adopts us as children, and not as second-rate siblings to Jesus, his true Son. Rather, he makes us "sons of God," inviting us into the same relationship that Jesus, the eternal Son, enjoys with his Father. This is why Paul uses the language of "sons" here as well as that of "children." It is not to give priority to male over female, but to emphasise that whether we are girls or boys, men or women, we all enjoy the same relationship with God that Jesus has. We are "sons," like *the* Son.

As children of God, welcomed into his family as one with his beloved Son, we are heirs of God. We inherit God as our portion in the same way that Christ does. As the true children of God, we will be glorified with Christ. Jesus has given us, as a free gift, everything that is his by right. He has given us the same eternal life that he enjoys: "And this is eternal life, that they know you, the only true God, and Jesus Christ whom you have sent" (John 17:3).

So, as God's children, we can embrace weakness and strength as Jesus does, remembering that suffering with Christ as we look forward to being glorified with him is our way of life. In the manner that the cross displays weakness and strength, we see weakness and strength working throughout Jesus' life and ministry, and so also in our lives today. As we see Christ's weakness and our weakness more clearly, we will see *him* more clearly, and understand better how to be strong as God is strong and weak as God is weak.

Weakness is not the traitor we take it for. Rather, it is our friend. Weakness can show us more of Jesus and how we may follow him than strength ever could. I am weak. But with Christ, we are strong.

3

Weakness Our Strength: Don't Run Away!

Our worry often lodges somewhere. When I am stressed, it goes to my neck, my back, and my teeth. These are fairly normal places, and you will know yourself where your worry goes physically. If you have had an injury in the past, it may be that the underlying weakness there provides a ready home for fears and anxieties.

The other place it goes for me is in my work. I am always busy. Serving a church full-time, I could be doing countless good things, but many of them will never get done. The freedom that comes with serving Christ so obviously and so directly should free me from any worry over work (we all serve him full-time, after all, but I have little excuse to forget it!). Christ is our Lord, and we, his servants, should learn that he is a good Boss who never asks too much of us. Indeed, he is the Boss who "came not to be served but to serve" (Mark 10:45).

Yet my general sense of anxiety seems to find a natural home in my workload. I feel overwhelmed, taken for granted, and put under pressure by the weight of expectations that others have of me. The fact that I am conjuring up many of these expectations from nowhere slips from my mind. Then, in a state of near-panic at times, I have a choice. That choice is where I sit.

In my study, there is an office chair at my desk with my computer in front of me. There is also an armchair where I tend to sit to read the Bible and other books, and to pray. When I am anxious and come into my study, I can seek Christ, or I can seek to be strong. I can sit and read Scripture, pray, and cast my burdens onto Christ. Or I can sit and seek control by emptying my inbox, organising my to-do list, and tweaking my calendar. I can sit in the office chair or in the armchair. The options for you will be different, but the choice is the same.

Worry is a constant element in life; anxiety seems to gnaw away at us a lot of the time. There is nothing new here, and Jesus assumed this sense of constant anxiety when he taught on these things at length as recorded in Matthew 6:25–34. Some of that worry is easy to understand. Perhaps you are worried about an approaching exam or a medical appointment. Maybe you know there will be cuts at work.

There is, though, a portion of worry that seems to have no clear source. Perhaps it comes from the way we are exposed all the time to news media about sad, wicked, and alarming matters. We feel out of our depth at work and overwhelmed by the sheer quantity of decisions we have to make about family life, leisure, food to buy, things to do. We fear missing out; we fear making the wrong choice; we fear uncertainty; we fear rejection. There is a vague sense that maybe we could mess everything up, or that maybe we already have.

So why do I choose the desk chair instead of the armchair?

Longing to be strong

I want to be strong. That is the simple answer. We all love strength.

We like the idea of being self-sufficient, in control, powerful, impressive. We watch sports that exhort us to be "faster, higher, stronger," in the original motto of the modern Olympic Games.[1] In the church, we know that we should care for the weak, but so often we seek to do so as the strong, the capable ones, the copers, those who have their stuff sorted. Strong people care for weak ones, after all.

The Lord's way is different. It is to bring the weak ones together to care for one another. This is often not nearly so attractive to us. For those of us who like to be dependable, it is challenging to think that we might need to depend on others.

A few years ago now, I was leading the team who were planting (starting up) our church in rural Norfolk. We were together one evening, discussing the sort of church we wanted to be. I suggested that we would not be happy to spend money on a holiday when a brother or sister could not afford to repair their heating system at home. I had expected some push-back: it was asking a lot, after all, to give up a hard-earned rest to pay the

1 From 1894 to 2021, the motto of the Olympic Games was "*Citius, Altius, Fortius*," or "Faster, Higher, Stronger." In July of 2021, the International Olympic committee agreed a change to this to "*Citius, Altius, Fortius—Communiter*," or "Faster, Higher, Stronger—Together." This new motto conforms more closely to a biblical vision of strength.

repair bill of another.

Instead, a friend said that he would find it hard to admit that he could not afford to repair his own heating. Most of the others agreed. To give up your money to help another person was a lot easier than admitting to needing help.

Strength takes different forms. For us in a small village, being resilient, dependable, and self-sufficient are highly valued qualities. In another place, strength would be measured in affluence, popularity or fame, physical courage, or intellectual ability. The university professor, the endurance cyclist, the decorated soldier, the idolised rock star, and the wealthy banker are all representative of strength in different ways. So too are the experienced builder, the unflappable nurse, the parent succeeding at juggling work, home, and family, or the teenager studying hard and also playing football for the school team.

In what ways do you feel proud when you look in the mirror? How do you seek to be strong?

Personally, I want to be in control. I am not worried about failing to excel at anything, but I am perpetually anxious about dropping something or letting people down. I want to be resilient, dependable, and independent. I want to be the sort of person whom other people turn to when they need help with a dripping tap, a financial need, or a season of doubts in their faith.

Despising weakness

Perhaps even more tellingly, I do not want to be among the weak ones who need help. A friend recently told me about a food bank at his church. On the mornings when the door was open to welcome in those who needed feeding, church members stayed away. If they needed to see the pastor or had some business in the church building, they would come at another time. This was so that they would not be mistaken for those who needed food, who needed help. They supported the food bank; they saw it as an important ministry. They just did not want to risk being seen as weak.

I am no different. Just last Monday I had a meeting at my home which was going to leave me just enough time to catch the bus to North Walsham and walk across town to the Bible study I was leading. It would mean skipping lunch, but at least I could keep all my commitments. I was also tired and going through a busy season, so was pretty ragged around the edges. Knowing this, one of the members of the Bible study group caught me at church on Sunday and offered to come over and drive me to North Walsham. As he hosts the study in his home, he didn't need to drive there himself (obviously!), so he would be putting himself out for me. But I was reluctant to accept his offer. I want to be clear: There was nothing but kindness and thoughtfulness in this offer from a godly man who loves to serve others. So why was I reluctant?

At least part of the answer is this: I do not want to be served, helped, or cared for by my brothers and sisters in church. In this case, I actually did accept the offer of a lift, but mainly because as I opened my mouth to politely refuse it, I realised how ridiculous I was being. I accepted it to be friendly, but part of me wanted to sort things out for myself.

How silly I am! We long for strength and we despise

weakness ... well, most of the time. (We will think about the attractiveness of weakness in the next chapter, for it does have a strangely compelling side.)

In saying that we despise weakness, I am not at all saying that we despise the weak. Indeed, I want to see my friends and church family freed from their suffering and weakness. Brothers and sisters at church and other close friends of mine are currently suffering from horrible weaknesses—the misery and fear that cancer and its treatments bring; the ongoing pain of depression and anxiety; long waits for operations to relieve chronic conditions. Then there are relational problems in marriages and families that bring their own forms of suffering and weakness. For most people, it seems that as soon as you scratch the surface, life is hard ... very hard.

I often seek to remove or undo such weakness by prayer, wisdom, counsel, and teaching. It is right to pray for suffering to pass—one day Christ will return and end all suffering. With his own hand, he will wipe away every tear from our faces, and we will never cry again (see Rev. 21:4). But to see the weakness itself as a problem is to miss how God is working.

We know how fiercely the world we live in values that which is strong, resilient, and sorted. God, on the other hand, does staggering work with weakness.

To see the Christ-given courage that cancer reveals in a brother or sister is a blessing to many. To watch with awe as dear friends smile and talk of God's goodness in one breath, and in the next one talk about how their depression is pretty bad today, can make it easier for me to trust Christ to hold onto us safely.

The weakness around me shines a light on God's work in many lives, and this builds faith in my own heart too.

To assume that the Lord's work always looks like health, wealth, ease, or fullness is to limit and misunderstand his glory. To assume that Jesus wants a large, rich, impressive, and relevant church that is making a great impact and leaving a clear legacy is deeply dangerous. When we think that God is found only in apparent strength rather than in weakness, then we are in danger of missing him entirely. And there's a danger, too, of trying to do the work of God in our own power rather than in the power of the Holy Spirit.

Sorted or submitting?

When we encourage others to serve in the church, we usually approach those we regard as strong in character, gifts, body, and mind. When we consider our churches, we try to address weaknesses and remove them. As leaders, we seek to be competent and to present the image of clever, organised, professional, and credible ministry. There is something good in this, of course, as we aim to use our gifts to honour Christ and share his gospel. But there is often also a desire simply to be impressive, or to encourage people to trust us for all the wrong reasons. We want our churches to look strong and successful.

Even our prayers can reveal our love of strength. This seems odd at first glance, as praying is, after all, a mark of dependence on God, asking for his help! Yet so often I pray for wisdom or for strength. These are not wrong things to ask God for. The problem is that they have become default prayers.

Perhaps I am on my way to a difficult meeting. A church member is suffering deeply, engaged in some pattern of ingrained sin, or facing a complex dilemma. I pray for wisdom for myself as I go to speak with that person. I pray for strength to stand for Christ if the conversation should become difficult or I am tempted to tell the easy lie rather than say the hard truth. This is not wrong. What is wrong is that often I don't also pray for the other person to know the wisdom of Christ, for Christ to be his or her strength, or for our Father to resolve the matter himself.

In times like these, my prayers have drawn dangerously close to using God to feed my worship of strength. I want to be the wise one, the strong one, and so I ask for wisdom and strength in me, from Christ.

In doing this, I can make my prayers all about *me*. I am more concerned with how well I serve my brother or sister than I am with his or her needs. I want to arrive at the front door as the one with the answers. Then others will see the sorted, together, able, gifted pastor. I will smile humbly as they tell me how much I have helped them. I will make them depend on my strength.

This is not what they need. They need a pastor to sit with them at the feet of Christ so that they might follow his gaze to the cross. There, in our Lord who died for them and rose from death, they will find strength and wisdom, weakness and love.

They will not, though, praise their pastor's wisdom to their friends or to his face. They will be left, however, with the joy and peace that come from Jesus.

Do you tend to do this too? Do you steer relationships to subtly make yourself out to be the strong, gifted, able person you want other people to see?

Coping strategies and shields

The other side of seeking strength is that we hide weakness. We might want to give the impression that we are on top of our work, our family life and home, our church commitments, and our relationships with friends. When we are struggling to keep one (or all) of those balls in the air, our instinct is to mask weakness.

Our friends ask how we're doing, and we tell them, "I'm good." Maybe they push a little deeper and say that we've seemed rather withdrawn recently. Instead of taking this as an invitation to open up about the conflict in our marriage and the loneliness it brings, or the strain with our children and the sense of failure we carry, we put up a wall. We say that we've had a bad cold, and it's probably that. We might well have a cold, but the partial truth is actually a lie, a shield to protect us from appearing weak.

While we pity those who are suffering, ill, broken, or weak, we don't want to join them. We enter an arms race of coping. We manipulate our social media posts to show the smiling faces and the making of memories. We hide the tears, the secret glass of wine or whiskey we need in order to cope. We hide the bruises on our arms or the pain in our hearts because we don't want to be *that* person. We really don't want to be the weak people that we really are. We seek strength.

But God doesn't.

God's surprising weakness

While we seek strength, God sought weakness. God sought us.

We have seen how Jesus voluntarily took on the weakness of the cross. And his embrace of weakness did not end there. He called a bunch of weak people to follow him. After talking about the weakness of God, Paul goes on,

> For consider your calling, brothers: not many of you were wise according to worldly standards, not many were powerful, not many were of noble birth. But God chose what is foolish in the world to shame the wise; God chose what is weak in the world to shame the strong. (1 Cor. 1:26–27)

Ouch! At school when two captains were picking teams in PE, I was always one of the last players chosen. But God chose me early on … and just as my heart begins to swell with pride at the thought, I find out that it is for the same reason! God chooses the foolish, weak nobodies. That's us.

But once we see that we are weak, and that Christ knows all about our weakness, then we will see that Jesus uses weak people in partnership with him and with one another to do his mighty work. Rather than building churches that are idols of strength, we weak people can play our small part in growing churches that are happy to be weak.

As foolish and weak people, the sort whom God chooses, we will see that the Lord uses us to plant churches that draw other weak people to Christ. We will see that he grows the churches that do not categorise people into those with capacity to serve and those with needs to be ministered to. We will get to be members of churches that don't have to project competence, plausibility, and success, and so become free to be loving, kind, gentle, and forgiving.

If we are content to be weak, then we will be joyful. When we see that Christ does not compel us to be or become strong, or to pretend to be strong, then we can breathe again. It is exhausting to feel the relentless requirement of projecting strength. To have a kind, gentle Saviour who was happy to be weak in his birth, ministry, and death is to have a Saviour whom we can know. In Jesus, we have a friend and a brother whom we can approach, knowing instinctively that he will treat us gently and kindly.

Breaching the wall

The wall of pretended strength that I build to conceal my weakness cuts me off from Christ and from you. If I want your help, then it will mean opening the gate, breaching the barricade. But as I approach the wall, I swerve away, turn back, am trapped inside myself and driven ever deeper in a desperate quest to find some inner strength. The longer I do this, the higher and thicker I build the wall and the more ingrained the habit to turn inside becomes.

But here is some truly great news: God is good at softening hard hearts and breaching strong walls. His Spirit gives us hearts of flesh when we are saved (see Ezek. 11:19; 36:26), and he goes on softening our hearts throughout our lives. One of the ways in which he does this is through our weakness. It is here that we see God's love and power, where we feel his closeness and kindness.

Paul knew all sorts of weakness in his life. One of his most painful experiences of weakness came after some truly impressive spiritual experiences which the Lord had given him:

> So to keep me from becoming conceited because of the surpassing greatness of the revelations, a thorn was given me in the flesh, a messenger of Satan to harass me, to keep me from becoming conceited. Three times I pleaded with the Lord about this, that it should leave me. But he said to me, "My grace is sufficient for you, for my power is made perfect in weakness." Therefore I will boast all the more gladly of my weaknesses, so that the power of Christ may rest upon me. For the sake of Christ, then, I am content with weaknesses, insults, hardships, persecutions, and calamities. For when I am weak, then I am strong. (2 Cor. 12:7–10)

This is the route we can take. We do not have to walk the path of strength and pretence that seems so natural—inevitable almost. We can be honest about our weaknesses. Honest before God and honest before one another.

Paul's initial response to his weakness was to pray. He asked for the Lord to remove this thorn in his flesh. We do not know what the weakness was exactly, but it was clearly something horrible—a "messenger of Satan." The Lord's answer to Paul's prayer is the astounding exhortation to endure the weakness by holding onto Christ's grace. We will return to this thorn in the next chapter to see how the Lord uses it to bring Paul through weakness to a deeper and truer strength.

For now, we will linger over the fact that weakness is meant to draw us to Jesus. It should bring us to constant, essential, desperate prayer. We are the toddler clinging to his mother's leg. We are the child crying out from the nightmare who finds her father's arms around her. We are the weak crying out in the darkness, and the King is running to our side with blazing light and strong arms.

We need to stop being embarrassed by our weakness and instead coax out weakness and examine it. For, as we said at the end of the last chapter, weakness is not the traitor we take it for. If this sounds challenging to you, then I understand. I have been brought low, and I hate it! But I am also learning to love weakness and finding it to be the friend who leads us to the despised and rejected One, the Man of Sorrows, Jesus himself.

4

Weakness Our Strength: Don't Hold onto It Too Tightly!

There is a sort of weakness that we *do* want to hold onto. This is the weakness that demands that others give us a break, that excuses our sin, and that allows us to step out of an unwanted responsibility. There is a type of weakness that we can hold onto too tightly, just as there is a type of weakness that we can flee from too quickly.

When I feel like holding onto weakness too tightly, the challenge is different. For those of us who already see ourselves as weak, the truth that church is a motley crew of weak people who need one another is a hard pill to swallow, for we can no longer sit back and let the strong, sorted people do it all, paying them the occasional compliment as their egos require. We are all in it together; Jesus expects and invites us all to love and serve our brothers and sisters. Whether we are "strong" or "weak," Jesus seeks to turn us back to himself and help us understand strength as he is strong and weakness as he is weak.

So why do we get weakness so wrong? How do we use weakness in ways that cut against the grain of Christ and the new life he gives us?

Weakness excusing sin

When we sin, we are confronted with an obvious weakness. We have shown a weakness in our morality, in our love, in our obedience to Christ. We have failed to live up to what people expect of us, and what we long to be true of ourselves.

To hold onto being strong and in control of ourselves and our worlds might mean that we deny sin. Perhaps, having been cruel to a friend, I turn aside his anger or sadness by saying that I was "only joking." If I *was* joking, it was at his expense and not in a way that I should have expected him to find funny. More likely, though, there was no joking at all, so my retort is just a plausible excuse for my unkindness. I have sinned, but my response that I was only joking is intended to say that the hurt did not come about because I am morally weak—a sinner—but because the recipient is weak, unable to take a little joke. I pretend strength by making my friend out to be weak.

What if that will not work? What if my sin is an obvious one? I came home in a foul mood one day and took it out on my wife, getting cross and grumpy because she had invited some friends over for supper when I had been hoping for a bit of space. When I later realised that it was I who had suggested inviting the friends over a couple of days earlier, I had to apologise: "I was out of order earlier. I'm sorry I was grumpy. It wasn't your fault at all, but I have been under a lot of pressure lately, and I've had a terrible day." I am admitting here to weakness, to being tired and stressed, physically weak. But I am doing so to excuse my weakness as a husband and as a Christian. I take hold of weakness to excuse an even greater weakness.

This is not a new response to being caught out. The first sin, the first rejection of God's Word, the first denial of God's love, and the first failure to trust his goodness came early. God had created a man and a woman and set them to care for his world, placing them in his garden in Eden. There was only one prohibited act—eating the fruit of the tree of the knowledge of good and evil (see Gen. 2:15–17). And they ate.

When the Lord God came to speak with Adam, the man, afterwards, this was his response: "The woman whom you gave to be with me, she gave me fruit of the tree, and I ate" (Gen. 3:12). The subtext is that the choice to eat what God had forbidden was not really Adam's fault. It was the woman who gave him the fruit. It was God who gave him the woman as his wife. Adam admits to being weak, but weak in being guided by his wife, weak in naively trusting God's provision. There is a lie to this, but also a grain of truth.

In fact, the man's told part of the truth, but even that was at the wrong time; he should have talked to God *while* they were being tempted to eat the fruit. He should have owned weakness *then* and depended on his Lord. He failed to do so. His character is proved to be weak, and so afterwards he hid behind the more acceptable weakness of being duped by his wife, and by implication, even by God. He was shifting the blame for the first time in history.

To shift blame involves admitting to some weakness while failing to own a greater, and truer, weakness. We would rather be stressed than mean; we would rather be deceived than liars. We want to be strong, but being weak can help us out sometimes.

Weakness as avoiding responsibility

It is not just blame that weakness can help us to avoid. Weakness also comes in useful in sidestepping our responsibilities. There is a wisdom in using weakness, the wisdom of the sluggard:

> Do you see a man who is wise in his own eyes?
> There is more hope for a fool than for him.
> The sluggard says, "There is a lion in the road!
> There is a lion in the streets!"
> As a door turns on its hinges,
> so does a sluggard on his bed.
> The sluggard buries his hand in the dish;
> it wears him out to bring it back to his mouth.
> The sluggard is wiser in his own eyes
> than seven men who can answer sensibly.
> (Prov. 26:12–16)

The sluggard is lazy. He likes to spend the day turning on his bed like a door on its hinge. He does not admit to being lazy, though; he simply portrays himself as being sensible. "There are reports of a lion in the village. It would be madness to go out to work just to end up as dinner for a wild beast! Far better to stay at home." Here weakness is used as an excuse to avoid responsibility. We all know how this works. We have all used this tactic ourselves, and we have all been disappointed or hurt when someone else used it to avoid helping us out.

Weakness as my identity

Worryingly, the sluggard, though lazy, sees himself as wise. There comes a point, however, when the clever excuses become just a bit too easy. There comes a point when we are not even sure they are excuses any longer; we start to believe them ourselves. We see this in Scripture when the Lord chooses a man to save his people from the destructive and unceasing raids of the Midianite army. Gideon is hiding in a wine press, trying to beat out wheat without any Midianites seeing, when the Lord comes to meet with him:

> And the angel of the LORD appeared to him and said to him, "The LORD is with you, O mighty man of valor." And Gideon said to him, "Please, my lord, if the LORD is with us, why then has all this happened to us? And where are all his wonderful deeds that our fathers recounted to us, saying, 'Did not the LORD bring us up from Egypt?' But now the LORD has forsaken us and given us into the hand of Midian." And the LORD turned to him and said, "Go in this might of yours and save Israel from the hand of Midian; do not I send you?" And he said to him, "Please, Lord, how can I save Israel? Behold, my clan is the weakest in Manasseh, and I am the least in my father's house." (Judges 6:12–15)

At first Gideon tries the same tactic as Adam—he blames God for the Israelites' predicament. When the Lord points out that he has come to help his people, and that he is sending Gideon as the chosen deliverer, Gideon shifts tactics. Gideon uses his weakness as a place to hide, just as he is hiding in the wine press.

The way he does this is intriguing. Firstly, he points out his family weakness. He comes from a weak clan. He has been born into weakness. No one can blame him for that, but surely no one can then ask him to do a great work. It is unfair to ask a person with a broken leg to run, and it is unfair to ask someone from Gideon's clan to lead.

His family is weak, and, secondly, he is weak within it. Perhaps knowing that weakness of birth has not stopped the Lord from using people in his service before, Gideon also pleads his personal weakness. He is "the least in [his] father's house." The youngest and smallest, the most often overlooked and easily forgotten. Gideon has taken weakness as his identity.

In a world that demands strength, there is a constant pressure to perform: work to be done, targets to meet, friends to care for, family whose demands never end, life admin that drops into our inboxes more quickly than we can manage it. Who wouldn't want to opt out? I have screamed to my laptop that I can't cope. I have searched for images of hotels in Spain and imagined escaping on holiday. I have stewed in angry self-pity, muttering that no one understands how unfair it is to put such pressure on me. I have sat in my study after work is done, giving the impression of being overly burdened rather than simply switching off my computer and helping tidy up and set out dinner, because I feel too tired to talk to my children. I understand how people end up permanently seeing and presenting themselves as weak. It is nearly as tempting as presenting ourselves as strong. Maybe that is why we so often mix the two in a toxic stew.

One of the most intriguing miracles of Jesus was when he healed a man who had been an invalid for thirty-eight years by the pool of Bethesda. Before healing him, Jesus asked a strange question: "Do you want to be healed?" (John 5:6).

Surely it is obvious that this man wants to be healed! He has been lying paralysed by the pool for nearly four decades. He must be desperate for healing. Oddly, though, the man's answer is lukewarm at best. He simply explains why he has not yet been healed. His lack of friends to put him into the water when it is stirred have made it impossible for him to gain any benefit from the hoped-for healing properties of the pool. He excuses his weakness with weakness. "I am still paralysed because I have no friends" is the essence of his response.

Jesus heals him, and this man's way of thanking him is to inform on Jesus to his enemies. From everything the healed man says and does, it seems as though the true answer to Jesus' question was a simple "no." This person did not want to be healed. Or at least he feared it greatly. Jesus' healing took away his infirmity, his weakness, his undeniable, complete, unarguable excuse in the face of any accusation that he was lazy or any demand that could be placed on him. Jesus' healing took away his sense of himself, his identity. This man had taken his illness or injury so deeply to heart that it had become his way of life, the lens through which he viewed everything. It had become who he was.

When I was a young preacher, I remember being simply unable to understand this incident. Now that I am in my late forties, it makes much more sense to me. The attraction of a get-out makes sense. This world is exhausting, and all the more so when we are trying to be strong in ourselves, to keep all the balls in the air at the same time. Rather than dropping a single ball and letting down my wife and children again as I seek to be the ever-available pastor and wise and present friend, the idea of being able to drop *all* the balls is quite appealing. The value of having a universal excuse, even at the cost of being paralysed, now makes sense to me.

Maybe you are stunned. Is Jesus accusing people who endure terrible suffering of using their weakness as a hiding place, just like Gideon used his wine press? Jesus is not accusing us, but he knows our situations, and he knows our hearts. The Holy Spirit has convicted me of using my weakness as a hiding place. Of course, just because I am easily capable of making weakness *my* universal excuse does not mean the same is true of you. But it is worth thinking over a little. Perhaps a way to consider it would be to ask yourself the question, "If Jesus offered me healing now, how would I respond?" What might you fear losing, even as you would love to receive such a miracle?

Maybe you are not stunned, but you are worried. You endure terrible weakness, and you fear that perhaps you have taken it on as a cloak and, as with the man by the pool, it has become very comfortable. Is there a way out of this that is not simply a return to our culture's love of strength, a strength you know you do not have? How can we rightly reject a worship of strength without simply replacing it with a worship of weakness?

Christ will help us here. He shows us what godly, dependent, humble weakness looks like. *That* weakness leads us to his love. It brings us close to him and his way of life. Christ gives us answers that will help us embrace our weakness as we should, and also turn away from holding it too tightly.

Weakness as a wayside inn, not a home

One of Jesus' answers lies in a similar healing. A few chapters later, we learn that Jesus healed a man who had been blind from birth (that is, for at least a couple of decades, given that he is now an adult; see John 9:1–7). Again, Jesus gave him a choice, this time by spitting to make mud that he put on the man's eyes and sending him to wash in the pool of Siloam. The man could have clung to his weakness, his blindness, and simply not gone to the pool.

Instead, he obeyed, and his sight was restored. Far from informing on Jesus, he then made a bold stand for his Saviour in front of the authorities. It was a courageous act that led to him being thrown out of the synagogue and welcomed by his God.

Jesus offers us healing and welcome. He offers us a better way than our own weakness or strength. Rather, he offers a path *through* weakness to a better destination. He takes us on to a strength that is not found deep within ourselves, but within him and in his love. We are meant to turn from *our* strength.

If you are weak, then that is in one sense a gift. Yes, it often feels like a burden, suffering, and a chore, but it is a gift because it shows us clearly that we are not strong. Our weakness is real.

But it is not meant to be all of who we are, nor is it the end of who we are, the final destination.

This is what Paul found when he pleaded for the Lord to take away that "thorn … in the flesh" (2 Cor. 12:7) and was told that the weakness was there to draw him closer to Christ. We considered in the last chapter how seeing his suffering through God's eyes left him boasting in his weakness rather than trying to be free of it. This is a far cry from clinging unhelpfully to weakness. Paul was not using weakness as his excuse or making it his identity. He was using weakness as a road to Christ. And that is what weakness is for.

Weakness takes us to Christ, and it also takes us to strength, to power. Jesus' reply to Paul's prayer was that "… my power is made perfect in weakness" (v. 9). In the dependency that weakness creates, Christ's power is made perfect. With desperate tears, the child throws his pencil and workbook across the room and sobs at his teacher that it is too hard. The teacher calmly draws up a chair next to his, picks up the book, and sits down, saying, "Let's do it together."

It turns out that "weak Paul and Jesus" is a more powerful force for the gospel than "strong Paul by himself." We might wonder whether a strong Paul depending on Jesus might be even more powerful, but our hearts tell us that strong people simply do not depend on the Lord like weak ones do. So the wise, humble missionary and apostle declares that he will boast in his weakness. He will lean into weakness so that he will also lean into Christ. This is the road to knowing Christ's power in our lives.

Weakness is a wayside inn. If you have settled down and made yourself comfortable by the warm hearth of being weak, then make room at the table for Jesus. Budge up and let his church settle down too. The wayside inn of weakness, comfy though it may be, is no place to live. Christ has an eternal city prepared for us. Weakness is where he meets us to lift us up and take us onwards.

We *are* weak and unable to travel the difficult roads of this strong world alone. But we were never meant to travel them alone. Our strength is in our God and then in one another. This motley band of Christians that you call your church is the strength you need, and you are the strength they need. Together, filled with the Holy Spirit, with Christ before and behind, you will surely find your way.

5

Our Weakness as Creatures

Parenting is a really good place to see weakness play out. Sometimes the problem is that our children think they are gods. The temper tantrum of a toddler who does not get his way (for example, when I tell him to stop eating the sand in the sandpit, a current ongoing disagreement) is an expression of rage against his limitations. He wants to be in charge, as if he were a god, and so to get his own way rather than having to obey me. In his heart, I am there to fulfil his desires, not to thwart his will. So being picked up and moved away from the sand offends him deeply. And he lets me know it too!

Just as often, though, I find myself lamenting that I am not God. As two children shout for my help from different rooms, I make a decision and go one way. As I face the questioning anger of the child I didn't respond to, I say testily that I cannot be in two places at the same time. I sometimes even say that I am not the Holy Spirit! When they ask me what the weather will be like in four weeks' time when we go on holiday, I answer, "I don't know; I'm not God."

When I say this, partly I am wanting to help my children see that they have a greater Father than me to rely on: I am limited, while their heavenly Father is not. Partly, though, I am exasperated by my own weakness. I *want* to be able to be in two places at once; I *want* to know everything. I wish I were more capable, more competent, more able to help. Often there is something sinful in this (and we will come to the weakness of sin later). But sin and weakness are not the same. There is an inherent weakness that comes from being creatures that has nothing to do with our sin. We are weak by design.

Made of dust

This creaturely weakness is a good thing. David remarks on it in Psalm 103: "As a father shows compassion to his children, so the Lord shows compassion to those who fear him. For he knows our frame; he remembers that we are dust" (vv. 13–14). The fact is that the Lord knows our limitations, and our weakness causes him to show us compassion. How different than a demanding coach! When faced with our tiredness, our failing strength, or our limited insight, Christ does not bawl at us to try harder, dig deeper, or somehow push through.

He remembers we are but dust because it was his hands that shaped that dust:

> When no bush of the field was yet in the land and no small plant of the field had yet sprung up—for the Lord God

> had not caused it to rain on the land, and there was no man to work the ground, and a mist was going up from the land and was watering the whole face of the ground—then the LORD God formed the man of dust from the ground and breathed into his nostrils the breath of life, and the man became a living creature. (Gen. 2:5–7)

The Lord spoke the animals into existence, along with almost all of the creation. Humanity was created in a particular and unique fashion, though. There was a humility moulded into our very being, as we were made from dust, dirt, or earth: we come from the most basic ground of life. Yet this simple dust was formed by the very hands of the Lord himself. His face drew close to the dusty face of that first man, and he kissed breath and life into him.

We are humbled and yet honoured in how we were made. Even before the treachery and tragedy of sin, we were created with a mix of earthy weakness and divine glory. We are made in the very image of God, and we are made of dust (see Gen. 1:27; 2:7).

Together, not alone

There is no contradiction between these two, as to be made in God's image is, among many other glories, to be made to need love. We are created to be loved and to love, to be dependent on our Lord, and to live in mutual dependence on one another. We see this in the way the Lord interacted with the first human. Already the Lord had blessed humanity and commanded us to "be fruitful and multiply and fill the earth and subdue it" (Gen. 1:28). One man was completely incapable of doing this. So it was no surprise that the Lord declared that it was not good for the man to be alone and created the first woman from out of the man's side (see Gen. 2:18, 21–23).

The man and the woman needed one another. The dependence that we have on each other is not a problem to be undone but rather a blessing to be embraced.

We see this around us every day. For instance, when you watch motor sports, the skill of the pit teams is one of the highlights. The driver is a lone gladiator on the track, but the pit teams rely on the intricate coordination of their efforts and practised speed in their work. There is a lonely pleasure in driving across the line to the chequered flag. Yet even on the champagne-soaked podium, the winner knows he did not triumph alone. He might enjoy the adulation his skill and dedication have earned him, but he is looking forward to sharing it with the team as well. We love to work in community.

Lonely achievement brings limited joy. Far more satisfying is the team win or the project seen through by the varied gifts of different staff members. Far less bitter is the setback or defeat endured with friends to commiserate with or colleagues to help pick up the pieces. We were created to need one another. We were also created to need our Creator.

From those first chapters of the Bible, we see the Lord giving the ongoing gift of life to his people through the Tree of Life. We see that, as well as God being available in prayer, it was clearly his habit to come and walk with Adam and Eve in the evening.

Presumably he liked to talk through the day just finished and the new one beginning. Humans knew nothing of the world that had been made except what they could see, and so they would need the Lord to guide, explain, and teach them how to care for it, as he had commanded.

God is a player–manager. Or, to change the metaphor, he does not give us orders like a distant general miles away sending a message down the line. He is the captain who explains what to do and then leads us onto the pitch or into the battle. The very way God made us is meant to reinforce our dependence. Perhaps most obvious in this regard is our basic need for water, food, and sleep.

We are used to tales of "mind over matter"—feats of endurance and impressive willpower. When we read of the regime of an elite athlete, the stamina of an ultra-marathon runner, or, in my case, someone who manages a twenty-four-hour fast, we can feel inadequate. Yet they all have their limits. If the tennis star does not sleep well, her Grand Slam hopes are in danger. If the runner realises his water bottle is leaking halfway through the desert, he is quickly calling out for help.

I am pathetically unable to endure any length of time without eating, but everyone feels slow and unsteady after a few days of fasting. We all have limits. We can try to avoid them, but at some point we all will reach them. We need to drink, eat, and sleep in order to survive.

This weakness is part of God's good creation. We even see it in Jesus: God himself, born as a perfectly sinless man, got thirsty (John 19:28), hungry (Matt. 21:18), and tired (Mark 4:38). It is encouraging to know that the weakness of being created is a weakness that Jesus chose to share.

It is even more encouraging when we see why God gave us this inherent weakness: he wanted us always to enjoy close dependence on him, to walk in step with his Spirit as a natural way of living. He wanted us to know the freedom of obedience to a God who loves us and enjoys our closeness. He does not resent our need of him: he enjoys it, because he loves us.

I can't be everywhere, but ...

Christ was not there when Lazarus died. He delayed two days where he was, and Lazarus was already dead by the time he set out (John 11:7–15). But even if Christ had set out immediately on receiving the message, he would have been too late. Jesus was limited to being in one place at one time, just as we all are. When he arrived, both Martha and Mary, Lazarus' sisters, said exactly the same thing as their first remark to him: "Lord, if you had been here, my brother would not have died" (see John 11:21, 32).

We see creaturely weaknesses worked out in Jesus' life, and these help us to see how good they are. Like us, Jesus could not always be there. This limitation Christ faced was a cause of great distress to his friends at times, even if it was not something he could be blamed for. We can hear the distress in those sad greetings he received from Martha and Mary. They had sent a message to Jesus to tell him that their brother, his friend Lazarus, was sick (John 11:3). By the time Jesus arrived at their home in Bethany, though, Lazarus had been in his tomb for four days (v. 17).

Jesus was not there when Lazarus died; it had taken too long for the message to reach him (Jesus could have got there sooner, but even if he had not delayed, he still would have arrived after Lazarus had died). We know this weakness all too well. "If only I'd been there." "I wish I'd been there." "If I could just turn back the clock." "I never should have gone out." The Holy Spirit can roam as he pleases, able to find us however high or deep or far we might go, and able to be in more than one place at the same time (Ps. 139:7–8). But we are not like him. We are stuck in one place. Just like Jesus was.

For Martha and Mary, this was a bitter truth. Jesus had not been there. If he had been there, they knew that his power to heal meant their brother would have lived. So Jesus was too late. Except that he wasn't. He wasn't too late to depend on his Father. He wasn't too late to love Martha and Mary (John 11:5–6). He wasn't too late to help his friends believe (John 11:15). He wasn't too late to do something more wonderful than the sisters had ever hoped. He wasn't too late to show them the splendour of the glory of God:

> Then Jesus, deeply moved again, came to the tomb. It was a cave, and a stone lay against it. Jesus said, "Take away the stone." Martha, the sister of the dead man, said to him, "Lord, by this time there will be an odor, for he has been dead four days." Jesus said to her, "Did I not tell you that if you believed you would see the glory of God?" So they took away the stone. And Jesus lifted up his eyes and

> said, "Father, I thank you that you have heard me. I knew that you always hear me, but I said this on account of the people standing around, that they may believe that you sent me." When he had said these things, he cried out with a loud voice, "Lazarus, come out." The man who had died came out, his hands and feet bound with linen strips, and his face wrapped with a cloth. Jesus said to them, "Unbind him, and let him go." (John 11:38–44)

By being weak and located in one place, yet strong in his understanding of his Father's ways and in his cooperation with his Father's plans, Jesus showed the glory of God. Our creaturely weakness is intended by God to display his glory. The glory of the player–manager is not in having a star striker, nor even in being the star striker himself. It is in the team playing together as one. Christ would have us so close to himself and one another that we are one body, and he is our Head. He created us weak so that we could be far stronger together than we ever could be apart.

I can't know everything, but ...

We are weak because we are not there, and we are weak because we do not know. Strangely, even Jesus did not know all things. When talking with his disciples about the day of his return, Jesus told them, "But concerning that day and hour no one knows, not even the angels of heaven, nor the Son, but the Father only" (Matt. 24:36).

Just as our inability to be everywhere increases our ability to see and show the glory of God, so our inability to know everything increases our ability to see and show the faithfulness of God.

Along with the other elders in my church, I experienced this wonderfully during the coronavirus pandemic. Early on during the stay-at-home lockdown in 2020, we held an online meeting. I began discouraged, having been unable to see most of our church family for a few weeks, and so I was concerned about how we were all doing. My fellow elders felt the same, until we started talking about who we had been in touch with. It wasn't just that between us we had spoken with most of the church family. Our encouragement came from discovering from one another that pretty much everyone in the church had got in touch with someone else.

There had been phone calls, messages, requests for prayer, doorstep shopping drops with encouraging conversations. In a moving display of the Spirit's work, some of the young children had made and written cards to people who live alone and had enjoyed encouraging replies. I was weak; I was not there, and I did not know. God was moving in his people, though. The Holy Spirit was prompting us to love one another in Christ. We were discipling one another and sharing the gospel with our neighbours. Together we had all the strength that God supplied and that we needed.

When I rush round with my wisdom and experience, able to fix this problem or help that suffering person, then all you get is me. When I do not know, and cannot be there right away, then you get my prayers, the help of the church as a community, God coming to you through his people.

We can sleep soundly

As the psalmist reminds us,

> Unless the LORD builds the house,
> those who build it labor in vain.
> Unless the LORD watches over the city,
> the watchman stays awake in vain.
> It is in vain that you rise up early
> and go late to rest,
> eating the bread of anxious toil;
> for he gives to his beloved sleep. (Ps. 127:1–2)

We can go to bed because, ultimately, the buck doesn't stop with us. The Lord made us to be unable to keep going. He made us to need sleep. The Lord so created us that for around a third of the time we are unconscious, not really there, and we know nothing beyond our dreams. We need to sleep, yet sleep is impossible if we must always be strong.

When I have to be in control, then sleep is terrifying. No wonder anxiety keeps us awake or sets us bolt upright at 4 a.m., heart racing and mind panicking. Unless the Lord is building and watching, then sleep is folly. But what sort of God would create us to need such a wasteful, unproductive, useless weakness as sleep?

Maybe a God who loves us too much to let us think we are in control. A God who knows the cost we will pay for isolated, individual strength. A God who prefers the strength of togetherness, and so makes sure that by ourselves we are weak.

So, sleep well, weak one loved by God. For weakness is part of your Father's plan. Weakness is our strength.

6

Our Weakness as Sons of Adam and Daughters of Eve

This world is broken. Like my tap.

It was past midnight, and I was lying cramped under the basin in our bathroom. I had changed three taps on two basins, and now, of course, the stiffest and most fiddly one was also the one in the corner with no room to manoeuvre. It had taken a long time to free the old, broken tap, as the nut had corroded over the years. It was taking just as long now to get the new tap to connect to the pipework. I nearly cried when at last I managed to screw it in place—only to find the joint leaking as I turned the water back on.

This world is broken. Not just my tap, but in deep and painful ways, things are not as they should be. Some of that is sin, as we see with weary horror yet again when the tanks roll and the screen shakes as artillery rounds land near the news reporter.

Some of the brokenness is not sin, though, but suffering. A friend read a comment online where the writer claimed to have lost his faith in God in a children's cancer ward. We can understand that. We struggle to hold together our knowledge of the goodness of God and the pain and suffering we see around and in us.

There is a terrible weakness in us, in the world, in our families and friends, that covers a spectrum from tricky plumbing to heartbreaking illness. This weakness is *not* sin, but it does have its beginnings in the first sin of Adam.

After Adam and Eve ate from the fruit of the tree of the knowledge of good and evil, the only tree whose fruit the Lord had forbidden them from eating, the Lord came to see them. He spoke first to the serpent who had deceived them, and then he turned to Eve:

> To the woman he said,
> "I will surely multiply your pain in childbearing;
> in pain you shall bring forth children.
> Your desire shall be contrary to your husband,
> but he shall rule over you." (Gen. 3:16)

The magazines show pictures of celebrities leaving hospital with their newborn babies, looking radiant with beaming smiles. It is amazing what make-up, skilled assistants, and airbrushes can do. My experience of maternity wards is of exhausted, ragged, sweating, confused, and messy people—and that is just the fathers! Childbirth is painful. Even with modern medicine and the centuries-honed skills of midwives, it is incredibly painful.

It is a pain full of weakness. My wife Flick is a confident

woman, and yet she talks of the vulnerability she felt going out of the house during the early days of motherhood. Pregnancy and the delivery of a child takes the human body to the very extremes of what it can endure. Caring for a little one robs the new mother of much of her sleep and takes her well beyond her previous experience and wisdom. At our church baby and toddler group, we are used to welcoming in mothers at the end of their tether, scared and unsure. They have, with courage, stepped through the right door. The older women know how to speak comfort and grace into such vulnerability, along with the offer of coffee and cake.

This is the weakness of a world fallen from what the Lord made it to be. It is not the only weakness, though. The Lord speaks next to the man:

> And to Adam he said,
> "Because you have listened to the voice of your wife
>   and have eaten of the tree
> of which I commanded you,
>   'You shall not eat of it,'
> cursed is the ground because of you;
>   in pain you shall eat of it all the days of your life;
> thorns and thistles it shall bring forth for you;
>   and you shall eat the plants of the field.
> By the sweat of your face
>   you shall eat bread,
> till you return to the ground,
>   for out of it you were taken;

for you are dust,
and to dust you shall return." (Gen. 3:17–19)

Adam was created from dust, from the ground, and so his sin results in the ground being cursed. As he raises crops and cares for the world as God commanded, he will face a difficult task.

I met a local farmer the other day. He was pulling out unwanted plants in a large Norfolk field that had been sown with rows of sugar beet. As we were talking, Philip told me the history of these occasional plants. Several decades ago, he explained, the farmers had planted beet seeds that had accidentally been mixed with wild beet. These wild beet plants look very similar to the cultivated ones, but they do not produce anything useful to a farmer. They respond to the same weather conditions and fertiliser as the sugar beet, and it is only as they grow that they become visible. In time they stand out from the rest because they grow bigger!

This means that they push out the sugar beet, requiring their own light, space, and water and thus reducing the yield for the farmer. They also seed, and so if they are allowed to remain, the problem will be worse next year. That is why Philip was spending days walking up and down the fields, pulling out these wild beets by hand. The technical advances in farming down the centuries since Adam sowed his fields have not reduced the sweat on the faces of the farmers who feed us.

We just can't do it!

All work is frustrating. We work hard on the report only to see the file corrupted or the printer fail to do the one thing we need it to do—print! We try to deal with an angry customer while the chef struggles to get an oven working in a baking-hot kitchen. We sit bored, waiting for the line to restart when the parts finally arrive, or for the traffic to move, or maybe for an email telling us we have been called for an interview at last.

We lack what we need to get the job done. It is hard. We sweat, and we grumble, and we rage at the stuck tap, knowing that hitting it with a hammer will just make it worse, but longing at the same time for the momentary release such an action would bring. We do not have the strength, the time, the skill, the training, the parts, the information, or the energy. We seem to spend our lives moving undone tasks from today's list to tomorrow's. And that is on a good day.

It hurts too much

And it is much worse when my head is aching or my throat is sore. The Lord told Adam that he would return to the dust once again, and that return has begun in all of us. We are subject to death, which means we are decaying towards that end and prone to illness along the way. We are on a trajectory we prefer not to think about.

This is a weakness that our current age in particular struggles with. A few years ago, I read a biography of Horatio Nelson, the British naval commander of the Napoleonic era. He is the most famous resident of Norfolk, so I thought I should know a bit more about him.

One of the things that struck me was how much time he spent

ill. Nelson contracted malaria as a young man and was struck down throughout his life by recurrent bouts of the disease. This was no impediment to his naval career or his fame. His was an age that understood that illness comes to us and that recovery takes time. We live in an age that sees illness as weakness and thinks that recovery simply means taking a pill.

This is why the coronavirus pandemic was such a shock to us in 2020. We had bought into the idea that science and medicine had more or less conquered disease. The idea that the world could be brought to a standstill by a tiny virus was confusing and unsettling. We are not as strong as we thought we were.

We knew this, of course, in one sense. We had seen the horror of incurable disease afflicting people we loved: often cancer, but there were other terrible illnesses too. Some required long, debilitating, arduous treatment regimes, or operations, or chemo- and radiotherapy. Some left us weaker, struggling and fearful. Others could not be cured at all.

These illnesses are terrible. They also render us weak. The weakness that chemotherapy brings on is cruel, hitting the sufferer physically, mentally, and emotionally, and also affecting the family dealing with the pain of someone they love so much. Then there is the added burden of hospital appointments and, potentially, the loss of income. The load placed on a family when a parent has cancer is enormous, sometimes unbearable. The desperate cries in the night are a reality we avoid contemplating, until they are forced on us.

Death beckons

Weakness will lead to death, the ultimate expression of weakness. The end result of being made from dust in a world that has fallen away from God's grace is to return to dust. And the only hope for the dead is the mighty resurrection of Jesus Christ. It is a sure and shining hope.

Yet it is a hope built on weakness. To trust that we will live beyond death, that there is a new heaven and a new earth where we will be bodily raised to sinless, unfallen, eternal, and wonderful life, is a hope built on God's strength to do what we cannot do. Only the Lord can give life to the dead; the dead can do nothing to help themselves.

As we approach death, we feel its weakness ahead of time. I am not an old man by our society's reckoning. I am forty-six as I write this, but my shoulders are stiff most mornings, my teeth ache too often for my liking, and I fear a return of the agony of a proper toothache from a couple of years ago. One knee sometimes twinges when I run. You know what I mean! Like an octopus, death's tentacles are reaching for my flesh.

It is so frustrating!

And it makes us angry. I see friends I care for deeply struck by cancer, and it makes me weep to see the myriad pains, sufferings, confusions, and tears. I have so little to say or offer.

I see the toll that chronic illness—physical and mental—takes on other friends. I feel the frustration of trying to work in a world where everything breaks and months of toil can be eaten away in moments.

Why are we so weak? It is because God has subjected us to weakness:

> For I consider that the sufferings of this present time are not worth comparing with the glory that is to be revealed to us. For the creation waits with eager longing for the revealing of the sons of God. For the creation was subjected to futility, not willingly, but because of him who subjected it, in hope that the creation itself will be set free from its bondage to corruption and obtain the freedom of the glory of the children of God. (Rom. 8:18–21)

Paul notes here that the creation endures futility. The very world around us feels the frustration that we ourselves know so well. Everything that has been created waits for a day when it will be set free from slavery to corruption, to decay, to death. The world longs for freedom, for glory; it longs for God.

This frustration was not taken on willingly by creation, but rather imposed: the whole cosmos was subjected to futility by God himself. But why would he do that? When you think about it, it makes sense that our groans, cries, tears, and rage against the weakness of living in a broken world would be echoed by the world itself. So we groan, and creation groans. But how can God have good purposes in all this?

> For we know that the whole creation has been groaning together in the pains of childbirth until now. And not only the creation, but we ourselves, who have the firstfruits of

> the Spirit, groan inwardly as we wait eagerly for adoption as sons, the redemption of our bodies. (Rom. 8:22–23)

Does Christ not know how hard this weakness is for us? Of course he does. He has always known, and so much more since he came and lived among us. Jesus never sinned, and so he was not subject to the fallenness of humanity. He did not *have* to suffer as we do. Yet just as he suffered the punishment for our sin despite never having sinned, so too he chose to take on our pain.

I have often wondered why Christ needed to be beaten before he was crucified. If he was to endure the judgement of God, to be hung cursed in our place, then why be whipped as well?

Isaiah tells us:

> Surely he has borne our griefs
>   and carried our sorrows;
> yet we esteemed him stricken,
>   smitten by God, and afflicted.
> But he was pierced for our transgressions;
>   he was crushed for our iniquities;
> upon him was the chastisement that brought us peace,
>   and with his wounds we are healed. (Isa. 53:4–5)

As well as carrying our transgressions, our sin, Isaiah tells us that Christ "[bore] our griefs and carried our sorrows." He suffered our sufferings as well as suffering our judgement. The wounds inflicted by the Roman whips were part of our salvation. He entered into the weakness of fallen humanity as well as the weakness of sinful humanity.

Jesus is not far from our suffering. He is not absent from the children's cancer ward. Our faith might struggle to see such pain, suffering, sorrow, and weakness, and yet it is there that Christ lingers.

But only for a time. God will not endure this pain and sorrow forever. The day will come when the Father sends his Son again. Jesus will return to end all suffering and pain. We will rise to life, or be transformed, to enjoy the new creation. The cancer ward will be emptied.

This world was subjected to futility by God so that we would know that it is broken, so that we would see, feel, and hate the weakness we are born into. So we would see who Jesus is, what he did, and how deeply he loves.

Then we will begin to long for his new world. We will stop trying to make ourselves strong, and instead receive weakness as a call to press forwards. On the long journey home, travellers do not stop in the wayside inn for the rest of their lives. They use it as it should be used, as a part of the journey. Fallen weakness, frustration, futility are friends to guide us to Christ.

Fear and trembling

And they guide us to him together. We need each other to keep following Jesus in a world that is so hard, ruined, and painful. We need each other, and we need God. Paul encourages the Philippian church:

> Therefore, my beloved, as you have always obeyed, so now,

> not only as in my presence but much more in my absence, work out your own salvation with fear and trembling, for it is God who works in you, both to will and to work for his good pleasure. (Phil. 2:12–13)

They are to work out their salvation together. It is a team effort. And the team leader is God himself, working in them.

Even before we sin ourselves, we are doubly weak. Weak as creatures and weak as children of the fall, we wish we were strong. Our weakness stokes fires of despair in our hearts. As we burn in impotent rage, Jesus pours in the living water of his own weakness. He chose to enter this weakness. To redeem it.

Could it be that Jesus can do more for, in, and through us, the weaker we are? In subjecting the creation to futility, could he have been preparing it for a more glorious and more joyful resurrection? He might just use the pain and frustration to strip away our self-dependence. If I cannot even mend a tap, what hope is there of my making a success of family life, friendship, work, or discipleship?

Maybe you will turn from this book to a terrible experience of weakness. Perhaps it is your ongoing treatment. Maybe your work is impossible. Perhaps the pain will not end in this world.

Christ will end it. He will come back, and you will live with him. And that day will be all the better for the weakness you are enduring now. More than that, though, today will be better. It will be better because, weak as you are and bitter as your tears may be, you need Jesus. And you know it. He weeps with you in your weakness, but how much more must he weep over the one whose mimicked strength causes him to push Jesus away?

The world is wrecked. The sails hang in tatters, too many planks have sprung, the pumps are overwhelmed, and the crew is panicking. Yet look at the Captain. His scarred hands are steady on the wheel, his whip-cut back is straight, and his gaze fixed. In his steady eyes, you see the hope of safe haven. As you keep your eyes on him, you know the ship cannot be lost. You will make that bright shore, and it will be all that you hoped for. More, even.

7

Our Weakness as Sinners

You couldn't see the infection. The rot, mess, and decay were hidden from view. The excruciating pain was written on my face and evident in my voice, but if I had shown you the cause, you would have looked into a mouth like any other.

I loved my dentist that morning. With a couple of jabs of anaesthetic, he delivered me from pain that felt like a slow-motion explosion in my head. I had already scheduled a root canal treatment for the following week, once the antibiotics had dealt with the infection in the tooth. But the night before, the pain had turned from a dull ache to agony. Painkillers had not touched it, so at 8 a.m. I had rung the dental surgery. Dr. Patel told me to come in straight away. He was ready with anaesthetic and drill to relieve the pressure on the nerve. In a few minutes, it was done.

Sin erupts in angry outbursts, violent hands, bitter cynicism, greedy grasping, exalting idols, and trampling on Christ. We can see sin, hear sin, feel sin, even taste and smell it in the world around us. It also lingers deep and hidden, protected and cherished in our souls and hearts. The outward appearance might be of health. It might even look like goodness or holiness. Inside, though, the rot can seep its poison through our bodies, minds, wills, and hearts.

It will kill us. Moses says that we should remember that sin will kill us:

> You have set our iniquities before you,
> our secret sins in the light of your presence.
> For all our days pass away under your wrath;
> we bring our years to an end like a sigh. (Ps. 90:8–9)

Our secret sins are not hidden from God. His presence in our lives exposes them. Yes, others might see the outward show; we might feel the inner hypocrisy and pain. But Jesus sees the deep evil. And he wants us to see it too. He wants us to see the totality of our wretched condition so that we embrace the totality of the treatment available. For the weakness that sin brings is one that he died to rid us of.

Number your days

In this psalm, Moses goes on to talk of the brief span of life, seventy or eighty years, and how we pass that time in toil and trouble. This brevity and trouble are a result of God's wrath at our sin, and so he calls us to gain wisdom:

> Who considers the power of your anger,
> and your wrath according to the fear of you?
> So teach us to number our days
> that we may get a heart of wisdom. (Ps. 90:11–12)

There is great mercy in the Lord letting us live so long in the treachery and evil of our sin: he is slow to anger (Ps. 145:8). But we must consider the power of God's anger. His anger is aroused; it grows. If we number our days, we will see that they will end. They will end in death, which is the wage we have earned by our sin (Rom. 6:23). Our inevitable decline towards death—whether sudden death in war or accident, the aggressive death of illness, or the lingering death of old age—should remind us of sin's poison, as well as of our fallenness.

This is wisdom which our age avoids.

As a family, we often enjoy a holiday in Canterbury, swapping houses with friends there. We have visited the cathedral a couple of times. There are magnificent tombs in the vaulted building, including that of the Black Prince.[1] The one that strikes me most, though, is that of Henry Chichele, who was Archbishop of Canterbury from 1414 to 1443. The tomb has two storeys or layers. On the top storey is an effigy of Chichele, resplendent in his majestic robes, with angels in attendance. His office, pomp, and status are clearly displayed. On the lower level is a second

1 Edward, Prince of Wales, was known as the Black Prince. He was a successful English military commander and known as a brave and chivalrous knight. The origins of his nickname are unknown but may refer to the black shield he used in jousts or to his ruthless treatment of the French people during his military campaigns.

effigy of Chichele, this time as a corpse with only a shroud to cover his nakedness.

Chichele had his tomb made during his lifetime, and set beside his seat. He spent church services looking at the contrast between his outward magnificence and the inevitable death that was working itself out in his body. He numbered his days.

Others of his era had a skull, a *memento mori*, on their desks. Then and later, church families buried their loved ones in the grounds of the building where they met on Sundays. They would walk through a yard of graves to pray, praise the Lord, and hear the gospel preached. They numbered their days.

Yet we'd do anything to avoid doing the same.

We move death into hospitals, hospices, morgues, and crematoria. We do not know what to say to the grieving. Bereaved people have told me that they have seen friends cross the street to avoid them, awkward and fearful of saying the wrong thing. We do all we can to preserve youth. We google remedies and procedures when ill, desperately seeking a third opinion or an experimental treatment if things are looking bad. We use make-up, surgery, hair dye, exercise, and anything else we can think of in our desperate attempts to recover receding youth.

Return, O Lord!

But we do not number our days; we are foolish. Drifting away from Jesus, and his truth and grace, is not inevitable. We can choose to swim against the current. We don't need Botox or cryogenic freezing; we need God, and he is not far away! The wise response to our sin, God's anger, and impending death is to cry out with Moses:

> Return, O Lord! How long?
> Have pity on your servants!
> Satisfy us in the morning with your steadfast love,
> that we may rejoice and be glad all our days.
> (Ps. 90:13–14)

Moses' prayer was answered. The Lord did return. He returned and died and rose. Those of us who follow Jesus have known the conviction of the Holy Spirit that we are sinners doomed to judgement, but also that Christ came to take that judgement for us. Feeling this conviction, we have welcomed Christ's offer of love, forgiveness, and life. We have experienced a union with Christ that means we have died to sin:

> We were buried therefore with him by baptism into death, in order that, just as Christ was raised from the dead by the glory of the Father, we too might walk in newness of life. For if we have been united with him in a death like his, we shall certainly be united with him in a resurrection like his. (Rom. 6:4–5)

Jesus will return once more, and then we too will rise. Death is conquered, and life is ours. Yet Moses prays that this steadfast love will "satisfy us in the morning," that we will "be glad all our days." We will still die, unless Christ returns first. But until that day, with Christ's life coursing in our veins, we can experience a growing strength in the face of sin.

Understand sin's weakness

We need this strength because sin makes us weak. The trajectory of sin towards death is something we feel even though we are no longer subject to death. There is a tension, a war, in our bodies as Christ's righteousness and life, the power of the Holy Spirit, subdues and kills our sinful natures.

Sin still brings weakness into our lives, and sometimes the connection is obvious. Maybe your body is weakened by years of substance abuse. Maybe your employment prospects are harmed by past sin. I remember an experienced businessman telling me about the sadness he felt over a colleague. This man had stolen from his company and had been caught. He went to prison, but on his release was unable to find work in the only field he was qualified for. Maybe there is weakness in your marriage because of the affair you had, even though it was years ago.

Perhaps the sin is not so obvious, though, and the weakness is more subtle. You feel like you are trying to connect with your husband or wife as you share a meal out. You are reluctant to entertain the nagging thought that your secret use of pornography, or unhealthy online shopping habits, or the way you join work colleagues in trash-talking their other halves, has impacted on you. Your children should be too old for temper tantrums, but maybe the seething anger they experience in your rebukes has taught them the way.

I usually feel like I am trying my best as a husband and father. I often feel tired and confused about how to do family life. I have noticed, though, that when I am close to Christ—reading my Bible, praying, enjoying the peace and joy that he gives—things tend to go better in our family. When I am not, then my sin spreads weakness and pain.

This truth about sin is pictured by uncleanness in the Old Testament. Uncleanness is not in itself sin, but it serves as a picture of the way sin works: by spreading. There are detailed and involved laws for uncleanness and for becoming ritually clean once again. Usefully, the prophet Haggai sums up the way it works:

> The word of the LORD came by Haggai the prophet, "Thus says the LORD of hosts: Ask the priests about the law: 'If someone carries holy meat in the fold of his garment and touches with his fold bread or stew or wine or oil or any kind of food, does it become holy?'" The priests answered and said, "No." Then Haggai said, "If someone who is unclean by contact with a dead body touches any of these, does it become unclean?" The priests answered and said, "It does become unclean." Then Haggai answered and said, "So is it with this people, and with this nation before me, declares the LORD, and so with every work of their hands. And what they offer there is unclean." (2:11–14)

This is how sin works: imagine that your boss humiliates you in front of your team by shouting at you for poor work that was not of your doing. Seething at the injustice, you take out your anger on your husband when you get home, criticising his sister who visited at the weekend in a way calculated to start a row. He puts the children to bed later on, and you hear him yelling at one of them who is messing around in the bath and splashing water everywhere. Your son goes into his brother's room and hits him. Sin spreads.

A slick of sin-driven weakness coats us. Our bodies ache, our hearts ache, our families are frayed, and our lives are embittered. We are forgiven, saved, and loved by God, but what difference does it make?

Here is the difference: he reverses the spread.

Uncleanness spreads, but holiness and cleanness don't spread. That was the lesson of the law, and it was true. It was true until One came who was so holy, so pure, so clean that he was able to absorb uncleanness and see cleanness spread. Jesus was able to touch the dead, and they rose to life (Mark 5:41). He touched the leprosy patient, and the leprosy patient became clean (Mark 1:40–41). Like the sun chasing away the night, Jesus had a greater light than any darkness of uncleanness, or even sin.

Kill sin

The weakness of our sin is a weakness we can fight. We have died with Christ and risen with him, and so we have that power to fight sin. We already know how to do so. Not alone, we fight with God alongside us, leading us, in us:

> But if Christ is in you, although the body is dead because of sin, the Spirit is life because of righteousness. If the Spirit of him who raised Jesus from the dead dwells in you, he

> who raised Christ Jesus from the dead will also give life to your mortal bodies through his Spirit who dwells in you. So then, brothers, we are debtors, not to the flesh, to live according to the flesh. For if you live according to the flesh you will die, but if by the Spirit you put to death the deeds of the body, you will live. (Rom. 8:10–13)

We kill sin in our bodies. There is a strength that the Holy Spirit gives us, a strength of God's goodness, warmth, holiness, mercy, and love, that is far stronger than sin. So you are tempted to lie. A friend has asked you out on Friday night, but you are tired and would prefer a pizza in front of the TV instead. Not wanting to hurt her feelings, you are tempted to say that you have already arranged to see your sister.

You could see yourself as facing a decision between a harmless lie and a night out you don't want. You could see it as a choice between getting what you want by doing the wrong thing or losing out by doing the right thing. The devil will tempt you to see the options as miserable morality or desirable sin. Christ wants more for you.

Christ wants you to be a man or woman of integrity. He wants your friendship to be reinforced with the steel of truth and trust. The choice, more accurately, is between being the truth-speaker you long to be or a liar. The Holy Spirit works in us the strength to spend the evening with our friend, trusting there will be blessing there. Or to thank her for the invitation but explain that we are tired and looking forward to a night in. We are on an inevitable path to resurrection life. The glory of Christ is our destiny, and one day we will know nothing of sin except the memory. So we can conquer temptation now.

We can kill sin! It is strong, but God is stronger. Feeling your weakness in the face of sin will drive you to prayer. Ask your Father to give you the Holy Spirit. Jesus promised he would do so: "If you … know how to give good gifts to your children, how much more will the heavenly Father give the Holy Spirit to those who ask him!" (Luke 11:13).

With the Spirit in you, what hope does sin have?

And if the Spirit in you is powerful, how about in *us*? The devil is wily in his attacks and has centuries of practice in tempting us. He especially likes to pick us off alone, ideally when we are sad, hurting, lonely, and scared. He knows well how to speak bitterness and cynicism over long decades until we are poisoned against our friends, our family, and our God. So do not be caught alone!

> Therefore take up the whole armor of God, that you may be able to withstand in the evil day, and having done all, to stand firm. Stand therefore, having fastened on the belt of truth, and having put on the breastplate of righteousness, and, as shoes for your feet, having put on the readiness given by the gospel of peace. In all circumstances take up the shield of faith, with which you can extinguish all the flaming darts of the evil one; and take the helmet of salvation, and the sword of the Spirit, which is the word of God, praying at all times in the Spirit, with all prayer and supplication. (Eph. 6:13–18)

This is a passage full of plurals. Every command here, every "you." Here is the squad of spiritual legionaries locking shields and drawing swords. Trying to fight alone with a heavy Roman shield and a short sword would be hard. To take on the dart-flinging hordes of evil by ourselves is madness. This is a call to lock shields with your church. Stand firm together. Pray, call out to your Captain. All the time.

Do not let sin decay, rot, and fester under the surface. Drill down into that tooth! Sin is common; it fills us with guilt. But Jesus paid the price for guilty sinners. Sin fills us with shame. But Jesus carried our shame on the cross. So we do not need to be embarrassed by its weakness.

To put it another way, how strong would we be if we would obey what James said: "Confess your sins to one another and pray for one another, that you may be healed. The prayer of a righteous person has great power as it is working" (5:16)?

We are surrounded by people made righteous by Christ. Tell them your sin, ask them to pray for you, and see the Lord heal your weakness and make you strong in the face of Satan.

8

Our Weakness as Churches

There was a disconnect that none of us had spotted—a discrepancy between what the advert presented and much of the reality it pointed to.

There were two opinions in the class. We had been asked what we thought of a marketing poster produced in 1999 to help promote Easter services. I was a theological college student at the time, and I remember the discussion well.

The poster was an image of Jesus styled on the famous two-tone portrait of Che Guevara. The text below simply ran, "Meek. Mild. As if." The subtitle: "Discover the real Jesus. Church. April 4."

Some of us disliked the poster. We thought that it was wrong to connect Jesus Christ with a communist and an atheist who had been involved in violent revolution. Others thought it was a good way of provoking thought about Christ, challenging the Christmas-card images of a clean baby in his mother's arms that many would associate with Christianity. I think I thought a bit of both. (I can be quite indecisive!)

As the discussion went on, I remember the lecturer making another point, and it stuck with me. He observed that we were considering the connections between Che Guevara and Jesus Christ. But the poster was also making another connection. It was connecting a radical, revolutionary image with a call to come to church for Easter. Our lecturer asked whether most British churches on Easter Sunday would feel edgy, revolutionary, and radical. That was a disconnect which none of us had spotted. The poster was not a reflection of the reality of much of our church life.

Or perhaps it was only a partial reflection. If you walk into a church, you will encounter two realities. Screwtape, the senior demon in C. S. Lewis's fable *The Screwtape Letters*, urges a trainee tempter to press into the difficulty we have in reconciling the two realities:

> One of our great allies at present is the church itself. Do not misunderstand me. I do not mean the church as we see her spread out through all time and space and rooted in eternity, terrible as an army with banners. That, I confess, is a spectacle which makes our boldest tempters uneasy. But fortunately it is quite invisible to these humans. All your patient sees is the half-finished, sham Gothic erection on the new building estate. When he goes inside, he sees the local grocer with rather an oily expression on his face bustling up to offer him one shiny little book containing a

liturgy which neither of them understands.[1]

Screwtape has a point, and it is one that he and his fellow devils have been needling into our hearts for centuries. They whisper to our souls that the glory of the church is faded and gone, if it was ever there in the first place. Or they hint that it is a sham: skin-deep. Sometimes it does feel flatly unimpressive, or more like the razzmatazz of the show than the splendour of the heavenly glory.

The local tearoom

Our church meets in the local tearoom. Come along and join us one Sunday at 4 p.m., and it will not feel like an army at war, the court of a majestic King, or the sacred assembly of the children of light, shining like stars. It feels more like a small gathering of ordinary people. We do not have the local grocer as a member of the church currently, but you will find a teaching assistant and a teacher, a building surveyor and a hairdresser. You will find people who are struggling in different ways. Some of us have poor health; some have ropey finances; some have marriages and families that are broken or fragile; some have deep hurts in our past or our present.

You will notice that the meeting starts late. There will be something that doesn't work quite as it should—this week, as the musician started to play, the images on one of the projector

1 C. S. Lewis, *The Screwtape Letters* (London: Harper Collins, 1977), 15–16. Used by permission.

screens were missing the top line of the lyrics. Despite my high-tech intervention of standing on a chair and wiggling the projector in the middle of a song, they didn't come back. You will spot that the meeting leader, preacher, musicians, and others helping with the meeting are very ordinary.

Impressive. Spectacular. Transcendent. Awesome. These are probably not the words that will come quickly to your mind as you spend Sunday afternoon with us. But hopefully, words like "friendly," "welcoming," and "interesting" will sum up your visit. Even better than this would be that your visit could be summed up by "Jesus and his glory, kindness, love, peace, and joy." It will probably feel quite ordinary, though.

I am part of a small church, and our meetings feel more like the picnic of a slightly disorganised extended family than a beautifully polished transcendent experience. This is probably inevitable for us. We do not have the numbers, resources, or talents to pull off a seamless, choreographed, impressive display. A larger, better-resourced church would have a different feel to its meetings, and neither is better or worse; they are simply different. In the large or small church, the heart of the meeting should be love: love for God, love for one another, and love for our neighbours. I am blessed to know plenty of large and small churches that have this love at their core.

Both churches can also get it wrong. A small church can make the mistake of perpetually apologising for what it is. A sense of insecurity and envy can pervade a church that always looks over her shoulder at her larger, wealthier, more talented sister. Of course, that larger church can have a parallel problem: a sense that it has "arrived" as people enjoy the new sound system, reordered building, or incredible musicians.

Both churches can take their eyes off Jesus. Both churches can forget what they truly are. For the deeper reality of the church has nothing to do with how outwardly impressive she is.

Terrible as an army with banners

The small church and the large church are both "beautiful as the moon, bright as the sun, awesome as an army with banners" (Song 6:10). This is Solomon's description of his bride, and in the allegory of his poetry, this bride is the people of God, the church of Christ.

Come to our church; come to the most impressive and largest church you can remember; come to your church. You come to a gathering beautiful as the moon. The moon is beautiful because she reflects the light of the sun, that great light of all the world. The church is beautiful because she reflects the greater light of the true Light of the World. As people come through the doors on Sunday, they do not come to a club or an event, or even to a mere family. They come into the presence of God himself. Where two or three are gathered in his name, Jesus is there among us (Matt. 18:20). Jesus is in our local tearoom on a Sunday afternoon, along with Broadgrace Church.

The writer to the Hebrews contrasts the church meeting with the great gathering of Israel at Mount Sinai. Moses had obeyed God and led the people out of slavery in Egypt. God had saved them from the army of Pharaoh, bringing them through the Red Sea to life and freedom. The Lord drew them to himself to show them what it would mean to live in the freedom and worship of the children of God. And God came in person to the Mountain to give them his law.

The fiery presence of God was so terrifying that Moses himself trembled with fear (Heb. 12:21). That day was as nothing compared to last Sunday, though. Moses writes that we have not come to that fiery Mountain:

> But you have come to Mount Zion and to the city of the living God, the heavenly Jerusalem, and to innumerable angels in festal gathering, and to the assembly of the firstborn who are enrolled in heaven, and to God, the judge of all, and to the spirits of the righteous made perfect, and to Jesus, the mediator of a new covenant, and to the sprinkled blood that speaks a better word than the blood of Abel. (Heb. 12:22–24)

The "assembly of the firstborn" is the gathering of the church. The New Testament word for "church" is simply "assembly" or "gathering" (more literally, "called out ones"). Here we are talking about church on Sundays. The writer shares the same understanding as Screwtape, but for him it is full of joy and wonder rather than the dread of the defeated devil.

We come to Jesus, and we come to his assembly. As we gather on Sunday, bump into each other in the supermarket, work together during the week, or meet up to pray, talk, serve, and laugh together, we do so with Jesus among us, in us by his Spirit. I live in Frettenham, and in the heavenly Jerusalem. And there is a gap between them.

When you walk into church on Sunday, will you see an army awesome with banners or the local grocer bustling up to you? You will see both, of course. The grocer, factory worker, midwife, bricklayer, pastor, student, unemployed person, and all the others *are* the "assembly of the firstborn." Both are reality, and we struggle to hold onto both.

So we try to close the gap. And that is a mistake.

Pixelated cathedrals

When we operate in our own strength, we labour to make the outer trappings reflect the spiritual reality. In bygone days, we built cathedrals of surpassing magnificence to show the glory of what Jesus has made his people. These days we build websites. We have apps, professional marketing, social media teams. We still have magnificent buildings. None of this is wrong, genuinely, *except* when it is done in a vain attempt to close the gap.

I love the glorious buildings of the church. I particularly like cathedrals. Indeed, I am choosing to write this book right now in the Norwich Cathedral library, surrounded by the craftsmanship of centuries of dedication to Christ. I enjoy the aesthetics of a clean and crisp website that hints at the beauty of Christ and the simplicity of the gospel. When all this craftsmanship, resource, and technology is aiming to serve the church and welcome in seekers, sufferers, and sinners, then it is good. Our heads, hearts, and hands should surely be used to serve our King with the best of the gifts he has given us.

So often, though, we are trying do more than simply serve

our King. We are trying to close the gap ourselves, aiming to create a church that looks and feels like Mount Sinai. We think it is up to us to encapsulate and convey the glory and magnificence of God. We build the most beautiful, technical, accessible, usable building we can because we subconsciously, or maybe even overtly, think we need a building that reflects the very throne room of light in the heart of the heavens. But the light, the glory, the magnificence shines and spreads from the King. Bethlehem's stable, Peter's boat, Martha and Mary's house, Golgotha's cross are all suffused with eternal glory, and Jesus lingers there. He does not need a cathedral.

We should not be trying to create a church that feels like Mount Sinai, but rather a church that feels like Mount Zion.

Mount Zion represents the place of crucifixion. Of the skull. Of weakness. Of resurrection. The Mount from which Christ will reign on the day of the Lord. The throne room of judgement. The heart of the new creation.

We can spot the difference between the two not so much by what we show as by what we hide. We might not have "Che Guevara" Jesus on our posters, but who is on our website? How closely does the impression it gives line up with the experience of walking through the door on a Sunday? Have we asked the grocer to step aside from giving out the books at the entrance because the new couple who arrived last month are so much more hip? Does the guitarist look out with love on his brothers and sisters as he plucks the first note, or does he gulp with fear that he might make a mistake?

Look harder

We need to look harder at one another. The glory of Christ will not be seen if we can just get a better PA system, a bigger building, or a more gifted preacher. The glory of Christ is shining around us already. It is there in the hand reached out to take hold of a neighbour's hand when tears well up during the first hymn. It is there in a hug that was the first time he had been touched that week. It is there in the tired eyes of the under-prepared preacher. Or in the tired eyes of the overworked nurse who is listening carefully to her friend's fears. It is there in the smiles, the encouraging pats on backs, the cups of tea held out that stop individuals from leaving right away, showing them that maybe here they really *are* welcome. So maybe we meant what we said about forgiveness and love. The glory of Christ is there as the grocer bustles up, eager to make sure this young new Christian is welcome in the house of Zion.

Jesus said, "By this all people will know that you are my disciples, if you have love for one another" (John 13:35). We should long for the glory, for the splendour, for the awe and transcendence, for the majesty. And that longing should draw us to our brothers and sisters in church, where it will be met. For Jesus is there, in their love.

Christ is seen in his people loving each other. This is the glory and beauty of church life. At a previous church where I served, we had a large number of musicians and were based in a city where several universities and a College of Music offered multiple music courses. We had one man taking a Ph.D. in composition, others who went on to work as professional musicians, and some who were not studying music and would never perform professionally but who enjoyed playing their instruments to varying standards. I am sure there were mixed motives, but I am also sure they all loved to play, to lead our singing, to see smiles and raised hands and the glory of Christ.

It seemed to me that however talented these musicians were, they all loved their brothers and sisters, and loved serving them. But it is not more honouring to Jesus to be super-talented. Nor is it more honouring to him to be average. It honours him to serve *with love.* That is where his glory lies.

So we don't need to close the gap; we simply need more eyes. Take more care to look at your church family. See their oddities, insecurities, poor fashion choices (if you can spot them, or otherwise join me in accepting that your choices are probably the poor ones!). Listen to their inarticulate attempts to talk of Jesus, their clunky responses as they try to comfort someone in loss or in crisis. Make sure you pay attention to every bit of food on their shirt, every rudeness from the children, and any sharpness from the parents. See how frankly embarrassing we are, and make sure you look closely enough at yourself to add your weakness to the pot.

Then open the eyes of faith and see the army, the assembly of the firstborn, the glory of the sun, and the beauty of the moon. See the church of Jesus Christ. And tremble.

The window of gifts

The gap needs to remain big so that we see the extent of the salvation that Christ has worked, so that we see what he has done in us, for us, and among us. The church is both churches: it is the embarrassingly ordinary and weak gathering, and the eternally glorious and magnificent Bride of Christ.

To look more closely at the glory, I have found gifts to be a helpful window:

> Now there are varieties of gifts, but the same Spirit; and there are varieties of service, but the same Lord; and there are varieties of activities, but it is the same God who empowers them all in everyone. To each is given the manifestation of the Spirit for the common good. … (1 Cor. 12: 4–7)
>
> For just as the body is one and has many members, and all the members of the body, though many, are one body, so it is with Christ. For in one Spirit we were all baptized into one body—Jews or Greeks, slaves or free—and all were made to drink of one Spirit. For the body does not consist of one member but of many. … (vv. 12–14)
>
> If all were a single member, where would the body be? As it is, there are many parts, yet one body. (vv. 19–20)

To see how love works among us as a church, and so to see Christ, we can look at the interplay of gifts. I rang up a church member the other week to ask how she was doing after an operation. She was doing well, eating a piece of cake that someone from church had popped round. The day before had been harder, but in the afternoon another church member had visited. She was encouraged that a few people had messaged to say they were praying for her, and the better day she was having was testimony to the Lord's answer. After a call like that, it is clear that Satan's legions have no chance. The church is an army awesome with banners.

It seems simple, although we all know it is hard to remember. The strength of the church is a strength found in Christ, known in love, and shown in ordinary kindness, encouragement, prayer, and speaking the gospel freely and wisely. Our strength is in our weakness, our ordinariness. When we try to find it in our performance or presentation, in the magnificence of our buildings or the beauty of our worship, then give the air a sniff. If Christ crucified is the Lord and love at the heart, then all is well. But if you smell the reek of human strength, the glory of man, or the pride of the eyes, then sound the alarm!

We are weak, praise God. We are weak together. And that is how we are strong.

9

Our Gospel Is Weak

Sweeping across the land, the conquering army moved with lightning speed. The opposing forces were crushed before they could properly mobilise, and the people were shocked and awe-struck by the pace of events. This is how we expect a mighty warlord to act, vanquishing his foes ruthlessly. It is not the only way to deploy power, though, as we have seen.

"Speak softly and carry a big stick" was the advice of U.S. President Theodore Roosevelt in a letter he wrote in 1900. The bully is more likely to give you back your remote-control car if you ask him nicely, and if you make sure to have your older brother and a couple of his friends from the rugby team with you. What works in the playground works in international diplomacy too. It is easier to negotiate when you have gunboats off the coast.

When you come with overwhelming force, there is no need to talk—you can just take what you want. But Roosevelt's advice is to encourage caution and consideration for your opponent, and to pursue an outcome more likely to lead to lasting peace. When someone has overwhelming strength at their disposal, these seem to be the choices before them as they approach their enemy. They can overwhelm, or they can talk whilst still making it clear that their opponent's survival is their gift.

Once, though, the mightiest of all lords, the Lord of heavenly armies, came neither with lightning speed in conquest nor to talk with the muscle backing him up. John's statement that "the Word became flesh and dwelt among us, and we have seen his glory, glory as of the only Son from the Father, full of grace and truth" (John 1:14) is extraordinary. Perhaps even more extraordinary for what it does *not* say than for what it does say. It does not say that he was full of *strength* and grace and truth.

Jesus left the stick behind. And he told us to do the same:

> After this the Lord appointed seventy-two others and sent them on ahead of him, two by two, into every town and place where he himself was about to go. And he said to them, "The harvest is plentiful, but the laborers are few. Therefore pray earnestly to the Lord of the harvest to send out laborers into his harvest. Go your way; behold, I am sending you out as lambs in the midst of wolves. Carry no moneybag, no knapsack, no sandals, and greet no one on the road." (Luke 10:1–4)

Christ could have called for back-up any time ("Do you think that I cannot appeal to my Father, and he will at once send me more than twelve legions of angels?"; Matt. 26:53). But he chose not to. He expects the same of us. "Lambs among wolves" is a phrase that has entered our culture. We talk about a student teacher's experience of her first lesson, for instance, as being sent as a lamb among wolves. When Jesus used the phrase, it would not have gone through the same cultural dilution. His hearers would have pictured blood, fangs, claws, and carnage. A lamb does not last long among wolves.

Not by the sword

This has been the experience of the church down the centuries. There are no Christian armies in Acts. No soldiers bright in mail with the cross on their shields. Before Christ's crucifixion, James and John had wanted to call down fire from heaven to destroy a Samaritan village that had rejected Jesus (Luke 9:51–54). Peter had drawn his sword to fight for Christ in Gethsemane (John 18:10). Once they saw Jesus die, and when they trembled as they touched his risen body, they grasped at last the weakness and strength of God, and everything changed. James did not call for angelic vengeance as he waited in prison for his execution. Nor did John as he went into exile, his last letters being a call to love. There was no sword in Peter's fist as he preached on Pentecost or in the temple. The record of the church in the book of Acts is one of amazing growth in the church against a backdrop of persecution.

Later on, things became more complicated. From the fourth century, when the Roman Emperor Constantine commanded his legions to paint the cross on their shields, there were attempts to spread the gospel by force of arms. But Jesus came "full of grace and truth," and when we bully, fight, browbeat, or control in his name, we cannot spread *his* gospel.

We deny the cross when we come in power. This does not mean a Christian cannot be a soldier—that is a separate question. It means we cannot kill *for Christ*. By all means die for him—and that is the honour he gives to some of his people—but you cannot kill for him.

Nor by the stethoscope

Be careful too when you heal for him. My grandfather, as well as close friends, combined overseas missionary work with medicine. This is a great sacrifice. I remember the openness and honesty of a retired missionary doctor as he told me about his temptation to envy as he and his wife ate breakfast in their terraced house in a poor area of the city. He knew that friends from medical school days looked out from their conservatories over leafy gardens, planning their day on the golf course or their next foreign holiday.

There is a sacrificing of strength on the part of doctors, engineers, teachers, and many others who head overseas on missionary work. They sacrifice a good income, job security, a respected profession, and a notable place in society. The danger for them and us is that this sacrifice might blind us to the ways in which we leverage the strength we have. When we go as the ones who know, who heal, who dig wells and build schools, then we go with strength. This is why wise missionaries have always sought to make themselves weak.

Hudson Taylor was a doctor who deliberately adopted Chinese

dress and customs as much as he could. This was an age when Britain was an imperial power, a global superpower. It was also an age when the norm was for Western missionaries to keep up the etiquette, customs, and dress of their home countries. Taylor, like many others, made a godly and bold decision. He took off the prestige and power of British identity along with his British clothes. As he tied his hair in Chinese style, he bound himself to the people he had come to serve. He left the safety of the British enclaves and the coastal cities where British protection made missionary work less likely to be dangerous. He used his medical skills to help and to love people, and to gain an opportunity to share the gospel. But he did so from weakness.

Wisely, the church does not connect aid with conversion. Whether it be the hospital in a developing nation or the food bank in a richer one, we help all, regardless of belief. We need to be careful, though, that there is no subtle pressure lurking in the background. As we are the ones who have, sharing with those who have not, we need to work out how we can make ourselves weak. God chooses the very people who "are not" (1 Cor. 1:28), so tread carefully when you "are."

So how do we choose weakness, move to weakness, make ourselves weak in every encounter and interaction? As he sat by the well in Samaria, Jesus made himself dependent on an outcast, marginalised foreigner. He asked a woman for water; he asked for help on a hot day (John 4:7–9). He could have tapped a rock, and the water would have sprung out. He could have looked up, and the clouds would have obeyed. How can you put off your strength as you talk with others? How can you follow

Jesus in this way?

One answer is that we can follow him with words.

Simply with Scripture

> And I, when I came to you, brothers, did not come proclaiming to you the testimony of God with lofty speech or wisdom. For I decided to know nothing among you except Jesus Christ and him crucified. And I was with you in weakness and in fear and much trembling, and my speech and my message were not in plausible words of wisdom, but in demonstration of the Spirit and of power, so that your faith might not rest in the wisdom of men but in the power of God. (1 Cor. 2:1–5)

We speak. That is all we do. That is how God saves souls, recreating the glory of his image where it has been vandalised by our sin. The words of the gospel, the message of the Bible, the truth of Jesus is the grace of God to us. God did not hide; he came. God did not keep silent; he spoke. We speak his words, his truth, his gospel. We speak the message of life to those who are perishing; we herald the kingdom of God; we proclaim the glories of him who called us out of darkness (1 Pet. 2:9). We preach, chat and reason with, persuade, and beg, even, those who love us and those who hate us to receive Christ who died for them. Words are not strong, but the Holy Spirit uses them to achieve what all the armies, wealth, expertise, and strength of earth and heaven could never do.

The preschool teacher had told me that the children were young this year, mostly two or three years old. She was keen that they should have a story to help them think about Jesus at Christmas, and that the parents might have an opportunity to hear this message too. After their delightful nativity play, I told them a story to help them see something of the wonder that God would be born as one of us in that little town of Bethlehem. It felt so little, so small, so easy to miss.

I sat with two members of our family in the sadness of grief. In the pain and confusion of their loss, I prayed for words to offer them comfort, hope, and peace in Christ. It felt like I had nothing to say. The gospel of Jesus Christ is not clever; it does not seem powerful.

We feel the folly of "the word of the cross" (1 Cor. 1:18). It seems unimpressive and of little use in the face of the torrent of suffering in our lives. It seems such a puny weapon to use against the evil and sin that we see spread across the world and entrenched in our hearts. Paul's claim that he is "not ashamed of the gospel, for it is the power of God for salvation to everyone who believes, to the Jew first and also to the Greek" (Rom. 1:16) leaves *me* feeling ashamed, because I do not quickly share his confidence. Paul might not be ashamed, but we long for more power, a more obvious working of the Holy Spirit. We long for miracles that fit our view of a mighty God better than patient suffering does. We want to see Lazarus called out of the tomb, not God laid in it.

Paul came in weakness and trembling. All he had was the message of Christ crucified, and even that he spoke in plain and common speech. No oratorical fireworks, no verbal gymnastics: just the gospel. Weak and yet full of power.

Scripture and the Spirit

The words of the gospel have no force or strength in them that comes from us, but they flow from our mouths as a torrent of spiritual might. Paul's message did not come with "words of wisdom, but in demonstration of the Spirit and of power" (1 Cor. 2:4). Luke records that Paul spent a year and a half in Corinth. He received a vision from the Lord there, with a message that he was to keep preaching the gospel fearlessly. Luke records nothing else obviously miraculous during those eighteen months. Paul was "occupied with the word" (Acts 18:5) and "teaching the word of God" (v. 11).

In 1 Corinthians, Paul said that "Jews demand signs and Greeks seek wisdom, but we preach Christ crucified, a stumbling block to Jews and folly to Gentiles" (1:22–23). So both from here and from Acts 18 it is clear that the "demonstration of the Spirit and of power" that Paul is writing about to the church in Corinth was not a *separate* demonstration from the speaking of the Word. It was not that Paul preached for a bit and then demonstrated the truth of what he said by healing the sick.

Paul's ministry in Corinth was explicitly one done without the signs that the Jews so much wanted to see. The demonstration of God's power was in the fact that he had the courage to go on preaching in the face of violent opposition, and in the fact that his message was received.

Clearly there were several times when the Lord did use

miraculous signs to confirm the ministry of the apostles and others in the early church, and Acts records incredible signs done by these missionaries. He may well work such signs today, but we do not need them. We are not meant to seek for miraculous power as though the preaching of the cross needed an outside verification or as though it had no power in itself.

The Corinthians' faith lay in the power of God to save them from hell, to forgive them their sins, to adopt them as his children, to give them eternal life, joy, and peace, and to set his divine love upon them. That power was worked in them by the Holy Spirit of God who rested on them, an incredible power given to them through the simple words which Paul spoke.

Warrior lambs

We have been given the same power, the same words. It is our words, as we come in love, that the Holy Spirit uses to give people everything Jesus is and all that he did for them. When Paul described the armour of God, he also listed two ways in which the church attacks and strikes back at evil. We are to take up the armour, "and the sword of the Spirit, which is the word of God, praying at all times in the Spirit" (Eph. 6:17–18). We are sent out like warrior lambs, armed to the teeth and ready for anything. We have the sword of the Spirit, and a direct line of communication to our Captain, who is utterly mighty.

There are two realities, two truths, and we must grasp them both.

In 1866, Robert Jermain Thomas offered his last Bible to the Korean man who would go on to kill him. There are disputed accounts of his death, although it was certainly brought about by the Korean authorities' response to the hostile actions of the ship he was travelling aboard. During his short life and brief time in Korea, he had given out many Bibles, explaining the gospel to anyone who would listen, and he died with little to show for his efforts. In fact, his life looked like a waste. The lamb had gone out among wolves: here was a naive young man stepping into a political world he knew little about and losing his life for his folly.

Yet the Bibles he gave away were among the means God used to bring the gospel to Korea, sparking a fire there that still burns to his glory as Korean Christians themselves now take the gospel across the world, as well as across their own cities, towns, and villages.

The lambs do not stand a chance among the wolves. Some of us will die as martyrs; others of us will lose our liberty or our livelihoods, a poetic way of saying we will hear the clink of a prison lock and not know how to feed our children. We might see our reputations destroyed, our friends abandon us, and our families disown us. The wolves will tear us apart. It will be messy.

But as they do so, our swords will stab far deeper: "For the word of God is living and active, sharper than any two-edged sword, piercing to the division of soul and of spirit, of joints and of marrow, and discerning the thoughts and intentions of the heart" (Heb. 4:12). The wolves will tear us apart, yet they will not stand a chance against us. God's words are more powerful than their guns or swords, books or censorship, cancelling or rejection. We speak the truth and grace of Christ, and they will pierce to the heart. The Spirit uses the message of the cross to save people eternally.

In your Bible, in your heart, and in your mouth, there is more power to be found than any general, king, or president can muster.

> For by you I can run against a troop,
> and by my God I can leap over a wall.
> This God—his way is perfect;
> the word of the LORD proves true;
> he is a shield for all those who take refuge in him.
> (Ps. 18:29–30)

10

Christ Crucified and Risen: No More Weakness and Strength

It just slipped out as the only thing left that we could say: "Come, Lord Jesus."

This prayer of certain hope came at the end of a conversation of mounting dismay. Many times this same prayer has been the only fitting conclusion to a discussion. Last night it was the suffering, sorrow, and weakness of a child in care. As I mentioned earlier, my wife and I are currently foster carers, and we feel something of the weight of misery dumped on children by families that are broken in deep ways. It is destructive and horrible to live in a family and a world where violence, abuse, and neglect have become normal, a misery compounded by a system woefully under-resourced for the growing need. All of this puts incredible pressure on the social workers, leading to unfilled vacancies and lost time off with stress and sickness. Staff are often working hard and trying their best, but the precarious system sways like a decrepit and dying tree in the gale. And when the bough breaks, it is the children who fall.

There is so little we can do. Bright minds and experienced managers have tried and keep on trying. Flick and I were not seeking to find an answer, but to express our frustration and sorrow, to voice our weakness and that of others too. And then to pray that Christ would come. This is the only way, really, to end such a conversation. And one day Christ *will* come. And that will be the end of weakness.

In both senses.

It will be the end of weakness in the sense that weakness will be over. There is a weakness that will pass, and we will never see it again, for Jesus will cause it to cease eternally when he comes back.

It will also be the end of weakness in the sense that weakness will have achieved its purpose and goal. This weakness will become true, all-pervasive, and eternal on the day of Christ. It is a strong weakness that will blend and unify and transcend both weakness and strength in glorious dependence.

Swallowing death

Here is a string of wonderful promises worth reading slowly:

> For this perishable body must put on the imperishable, and this mortal body must put on immortality. When the perishable puts on the imperishable, and the mortal puts on immortality, then shall come to pass the saying that is written:
>
> "Death is swallowed up in victory."

"O death, where is your victory?
O death, where is your sting?" (1 Cor. 15:53–55)

Our bodies are perishable by nature. Given over to death by Adam's sin, and hastened to our ruin by our own headlong rush to live out the sin we are born with, we are like the toys in the film *Toy Story 3*. One problem after another has led the toys into a furnace. They try to climb out, but the mountain of rubbish they are slithering down is too steep and too unstable to climb. They slide inexorably towards the fire. With no hope of escape, the toys take one another's hands for comfort as they wait for the flames.

Their predicament is a fair picture of ours. We are sliding inescapably towards death. Our aches and illnesses give us unwelcome reminders of what is to come. I tend to think of the toys as being like the church. We take hold of each other's hands, living in this broken and fallen world by offering love to one another, stretching out to draw in anyone we can to our family. And we hold hands as we slip together towards the inevitable.

And then the little toy aliens make it to the control room, unknown to the toys, and use an enormous crane to scoop their friends to safety. The church is rescued too, though not through any strength of her own. But not unlike the end for the toys, the future of God's friends is not in the furnace but in a rescue: "This perishable body must put on the imperishable." Christ will come back for us.

We will be raised from the dead. Not with the same bodies as we have now, but with transformed bodies. The sinful nature, our bent towards selfishness and cruelty, will be utterly gone. With it we will shed our trajectory towards death and instead be curved eternally towards life and light.

Older folk I know have their characters etched on their faces. There is a deep beauty to a face marked with the laughter of decades, with tears shed for real sadnesses, and with a brow furrowed from earnest prayer and shared sorrows. That beauty is mingled these days with the decay of ageing. The slide towards death and the grasping tentacles of entropy mark us younger ones too. But what will it look like to gaze on a ninety-two-year-old man in his resurrection body, all signs of sin and death gone and only the marks of good tears and good laughter left? The beauty would floor us if we saw it. What will that man look like after a thousand years in Christ's presence?

The weakness of our fallen state, and of our sin itself, will be gone forever. Victory swallows up death.

Even here, though, where we see a move from weakness to strength, it is only because of weakness and through weakness that this strength can come. Christ died in weakness to rise in glorious victory and vindication. God his Father raised him from the dead, so vindicating him and showing that he truly is the righteous, obedient, glorious, and eternal Son of God and promised Messiah. The curse, judgement, death, and humiliation that he took on himself was truly his. It was truly his by love, though, not because he deserved it.

Jesus rode a donkey through the gates of Jerusalem, arriving in humble peace rather than prestigious triumph. But he did not treat the gates of death so gently! He smashed them to splinters and carried off their frame and bars. He left death ransacked and plundered, her sting taken and her power broken.

His weakness and strength paved the way for us to see our need, our dependence on a Saviour. We are weak, and by showing us our helplessness, the Holy Spirit has opened our eyes to see Jesus' rescue.

Death has no victory—the weakness of our fallen state, of our inherited guilt, of our inevitable death is completely undone. Death also has no sting. Paul goes on to say that "the power of sin is the law"—i.e., the ways that we break God's good and holy commands. The "sting of death is [our] sin" (1 Cor. 15:56), and when our sin is gone, death no longer becomes the confirmation of our utter weakness, but instead the doorway to life in Christ. Even as we die, weaker than we have ever been, we are welcomed into the warm light of the love of God. We are stronger than ever.

Strength giving way to strength

"Truly, I say to you, whoever says to this mountain, 'Be taken up and thrown into the sea,' and does not doubt in his heart, but believes that what he says will come to pass, it will be done for him" (Mark 11:23). I am not so free of doubt to take fully this promise of Christ. I cannot move the mountain into the sea.

Jesus says that we can move mountains simply with undoubting belief. This is not a party trick, or even a superpower to be used when we see the need. Jesus is talking about the power of faith in doing what God desires and commands. It feels harder than shifting mountains—give me enough time and a mechanical digger, and I could maybe do that. I do not have to shift a mountain, though, as I have a far harder task: I have to go back to normal life.

It is the summer school holidays as I write. I am tired and have noticed in my life an increasing tendency to get angry and bitter. I know that the happy road of repentance leads me to stop depending on my own limited abilities and to rely on God. I can grow in dependence on God by practising thanksgiving for his many gifts and blessings. Through constant prayer for the many needs I see around me, I can set my heart to respond to suffering and stress with dependent trust. But I am still struggling with a sense of hopelessness.

I had thought that the summer would give a chance for rest, which it has done. I was looking forward to some days spent writing in the library of Norwich Cathedral, which I am now doing. I had thought that all my tiredness and stress from the last few pandemic-scarred years would fall away, and I would enter the new academic year as a new man. That has not happened.

My body aches, and my mind feels like a wasps' nest of buzzing, stinging needs, tasks, concerns, and distractions. There are two possibilities for the next few weeks. My track record in trusting the Lord in the face of the worries and anxieties of the world is, frankly, not great. My prayer life is shabby, and my thankfulness late, seldom, and grudging. So my bitter fear is that when the new term starts and all the busyness and work piles on again, I will simply become more angry and bitter.

The other possibility is that Christ's grace is sufficient for me, that his love is greater than my sin. Underneath the layers of fear and worry, there is the hope that Jesus will give me faith to move mountains. This hope is certain. And the fear is not.

The hope is certain because one day it will be the *only* reality: "When Christ who is your life appears, then you also will appear with him in glory" (Col. 3:4). Christ is my life now, but when he returns to earth, we will live with him. We will be risen to new life, as he is. We will enjoy his glory and share it. We will depend entirely on the Holy Spirit's work in our hearts, and on Jesus who is our glorious Head, and on our Father who has adopted us and cares so well for his children. The idea of independent strength will seem ludicrous, sickening even, to us. The knowledge that we used to pursue it so vehemently and worship it with such devotion will appal and maybe intrigue us.

We are creatures, made to live dependent lives of freedom, peace, and joy in the company of God. On that first day, Adam and Eve were not pioneers, striving together against a hostile world and conquering all before them. They were happy gardeners working with delicious anticipation for the cool of the day, when the Lord would come and walk with them and they would eagerly tell him what they had done and plan the next day together. We are not the Lone Ranger; we are children at play in the garden of God.

When Jesus returns, this creaturely weakness will not end: it will be perfected. We will revel in our need and the ways that our Father meets it more kindly and fully than we had expected or imagined. We will be completely strong, with all the infinite strength of the Trinity. God's power and the mutual dependence of Father, Son, and Spirit will be the beat of our hearts and the inclination of our wills. Weakness and strength will both be transfigured and restored to what they should be—dependence.

As weak now as we will be then

The verses just before that promise of our appearing in glory when Christ appears are not directed to this great future hope, however. Paul writes,

> If then you have been raised with Christ, seek the things that are above, where Christ is, seated at the right hand of God. Set your minds on things that are above, not on things that are on earth. For you have died, and your life is hidden with Christ in God. (Col. 3:1–3)

The certainty of our future resurrection dictates the sort of hope we now enjoy. It is the living hope of the work of God's Spirit in our lives to bring us to that final resurrection. We are not only waiting to be raised with Christ, but we enjoy that resurrection now. This is why I can hope in Christ despite my past sins and present stresses. We have been raised with Christ to life just as surely as we have died with him to sin. Our life is not only the obvious going to work or school, coming home, cooking dinner, arguing, complaining, grasping, and begrudging. Our life, more truly and fully, is hidden to most but seen by angels, and by us if we are wise. Our life is in Christ. And we grow by fixing our minds on heavenly things.

Battered by waves, spray stinging their eyes, the fishermen pulled hard on the oars. They were exhausted and making little progress against the gale. Through the waves, they glimpsed a man walking across the sea. Fearing a ghost, they screamed. Then Jesus—for it was he—called out to comfort them. For the Lord who rides on the wings of the storm, it is not a hard matter to walk the paths of the sea.

Brave Peter asked the Lord to command him to come to him on the waters, and Jesus did so. Peter, a man like us, walked over the waves to his Lord. The others held their breath as Peter stumbled. Seeing the ferocity of the wind and realising the impossibility of his walk, he began to be terribly afraid. As doubts flooded his heart, he felt the water on his legs. With rising dread, he began to sink and flounder.

As death reached for him, he cried out, "Lord, save me" (Matt. 14:30). Instead of the cold hand of a watery grave, it was Christ who took hold of him.

We are destined for life with Jesus. Our weakness and strength will one day give way to happy dependence. Today, we can look at the waves, or we can keep our eyes on the love in Christ's gaze. And when we sink, we only need Peter's simple prayer: "Lord, save me," and we will feel the nail-marked hand taking hold of us again.

That is a good way to finish a chapter. But maybe it is too good. Is it really that easy?

Does God really come to help us in the middle of a family argument when everyone is shouting and most of us are crying? Can Jesus really save us as we stare at the exam paper with empty minds and rising panic? Does that prayer make any difference as the boss says, "I'm sorry …" or the jury declares us guilty, the doctor confirms our fears or our brother rings with terrible news?

It feels bold to say that it is true. That Jesus is there in the storm with his hand held out time and again. But that has been my experience. You cannot, should not, and must not, though, give my experience much weight in your faith. So trust Jesus, and try it for yourself. He is not far; he is not slow; he does love and care; he understands and works more deeply and powerfully than you can see. He will probably not answer as you expect, but he will be there; he will answer, and his love will shine. So pray Peter's prayer when you have no other words left: "Lord, save me."

He will do. And one day he will embrace you physically. He will wipe your eyes and take your hand, and it will all be well.

Amen. Come, Lord Jesus.

CONCLUSION

Don't Fear Weakness

Jesus would not have made us weak if we were meant to be strong. He would not have redeemed us in weakness if he had valued strength more highly. Our Father would not have tolerated the ways we treated and treat his Son if he were a God of strength and might alone. The Holy Spirit would not endure living and working in, and with, such poor material as we are if he were only after productivity, impressive results, or a spectacular impact. God did not seem to want strength when he created the cosmos.

Now, you might have noticed a strange gap in the book so far. For it's true—there are times when the Lord does give his people spectacular strength. There was the literal strength he gave to Samson to single-handedly defeat a great force of enemy warriors, armed only with the jawbone of a donkey (Judg. 15:14–17). Then there was the sort of political and financial strength he gave to King Solomon (1 Kings 10). Just as amazing was the strength of courage and faith he gave to the apostles to speak the truth of Christ under threat of death (as in Acts 4:13).

Maybe you have experienced such supernatural strength. I have. I well remember the phone call late on a Sunday night when a friend was not sure whether to do one thing or another. There was no way I could see to decide, and then the Holy Spirit convicted me with utter certainty of the right course to advise. I told my friend I thought this was from God. He followed my advice, and we later found out that it would have been a disaster if he had not done so. Of course we did not know that at the time, but God did.

We must not miss these times of miraculous strength. They are great gifts to us now, as they were to the believers in Bible times. The reason we have neglected them in this book is that they don't surprise us. The idea that God might give great strength to help us is one we easily accept. We understand that God does not fear or despise strength. But to come back to the core theme of this book, the wonder is that he doesn't fear or despise weakness either.

If God does not fear or despise weakness, then it follows that we shouldn't. To be blunt: don't fear weakness.

Maybe you are already persuaded. The Lord has dismantled your desire for strength and brought you to see that weakness really is not to be feared but to be followed. Weakness is a guide to Christ, a friend who invites us into dependence on a God who is completely dependable.

But how do you live that out? What does it look like to embrace weakness and not despise it?

You will have ideas and thoughts from what you have read and what the Holy Spirit has sparked within you in your particular situation. This might be a good point to spend some time praying over them. It would also be worth considering jotting some notes down to ponder yourself or discuss with others so that you get the chance to sink good roots deeper into your heart. Here are some ideas from my experience.

Share

Weakness is meant to make us dependent. So depend! Share your weakness. You have friends, brothers, and sisters at church who are worth trusting. Maybe jot down a few weaknesses you are struggling with. Think about your weakness as a creature, as a fallen person, as a sinner. Be open and straightforward. Maybe you can share in a church group you are part of or arrange a coffee with a friend. Go for a walk with a couple of people you trust and admit how you are struggling. Turn away from trying to look strong by instead being open and honest about your weakness.

I reckon you will not be the only one sharing in that conversation. I also reckon your friends will have some pretty powerful ways to shine gospel light into your weakness. You will have things to tell them too, or remind them of. There will be blessing, love, relief, and freedom in that conversation. You will need to order a second coffee. You will need to walk another lap. Jesus may well work things out in ways which you cannot even guess possible at this stage.

Read

Put the weakness of God at the forefront of your mind as you read the Bible. That may sound odd, as we have seen that he is both strong and weak. I think we tend to remember the strength more easily, though. We see the strength of God as he guides the stone from the hand of the shepherd boy to slay the mighty giant and save his people. But God acts through the weakness of faith flying in the face of facts. He acts in grace, giving not only Israel but the army of the Philistines a chance to see that true strength lies in weakness.

When you read the Bible, you see that God does not fear seeming weak or being weak. He prefers to love than to win. And then he wins through love that looks embarrassingly like defeat! He is strange, wonderful, and better than I make him out to be, and he is everything I need him to be, and more. Read the Bible to see a weak Christ, and you will find you are not imposing him on the text, but maybe you are seeing a facet of God you have missed before. He is lovely to behold!

Pray

Pray. Pray. Pray.

This must be the heart of dependence, the meeting point of godly weakness and godly strength. We talk about prayer a lot; we have books on prayer and apps to order our prayer lives. But we just don't do it very much. Prayer is simply talking to God and laying our needs before him. Asking.

Thanksgiving is the necessary flip side. As we see how our Father has answered our prayers, we naturally thank him for doing so, and then we pray in faith and confidence that he is no different now in his love and power than he was when we made our request. Jesus is kind, and so showing us our weakness through this book will be one way that he draws us closer to his Father. That will work itself out in many ways, but not least in our prayer lives. Pray as if everything depended on God. It does!

Laugh

Laughing at ourselves, and joining with others to laugh together at our weaknesses, is powerful. As elders in our church, we sometimes talk about our weaknesses, even our proneness to sin and folly, in a hyperbolic manner. I might say something like this: "Can you pray for me, brothers? I am taking Flick for granted and being cold towards her. I don't even really know why—I guess it is because I am a god who deserves to be worshipped." One of the others might reply like this: "Doesn't she realise what a mighty god you are, and how lucky she is to be able to worship you?" And we laugh at my pride and folly before we pray.

This means that we pray with a sense of our ridiculous stupidity. Our sin is not noble; it is not profound. It is as silly as the sort of thing you see in the school playground. It is as wicked, grubby, and mean as the sort of thing you see in the courtroom. Laughing at ourselves can be humbling in a wholesome sort of way.

Of course, much sin has nothing of laughter in it at all, and different cultures will laugh at themselves in different ways. We need to be careful when we laugh and how, but just remember that God is not glum!

Long

Whether your weakness can be laughed at, or whether it is so deep and terrible a suffering that the only right response is weeping and waiting, it is not the end. The tears will pass, even though they are constant now, and the horror will end. The terror will be gone in the dawning of the day of Christ, and the pain will be washed away in the river of life.

Like a climber who has slipped, we hold on for dear life, and we know that our grip is failing, our arms are weak, and our handhold is loose. We feel the desperation of weakness, and our panic is rising.

Perhaps you read the section on laughing just now with a bitter snarl. You are right that I do not understand, that I would never have written that if I were in your shoes. I am sorry. But you also know that Jesus does understand. Maybe there is a part of you that tries to deny even that, for you fear to hope again. But the cross is too stark, too bloody, too naked, too accursed, and too shameful for you to push away the love of Christ for you. His love is displayed there. He died for you; he loves us more deeply and truly than any of us can ever grasp.

As your grip finally gives way, please know that you will not perish on the jagged rocks of despairing weakness. Almost against yourself, know that you will fall into the arms of God.

Amen. Come, Lord Jesus.

SCRIPTURE INDEX

OLD TESTAMENT

NEW TESTAMENT

ALSO AVAILABLE FROM
UNION PUBLISHING

GIVEAWAY

RECEIVE FREE
RESOURCES EVERY
MONTH WHEN YOU
SUBSCRIBE TO
UNION PUBLISHING.